THE NEW CLASSIC HOME

MODERN MEETS TRADITIONAL STYLE

PALOMA CONTRERAS

FOREWORD BY INDIA HICKS

TEXT BY
KATHRYN O'SHEA-EVANS

WITH PRINCIPAL PHOTOGRAPHY BY
AIMÉE MAZZENGA

ABRAMS, NEW YORK

To Fabian and Margot—
you make life more beautiful.

CONTENTS

AS A CHILD I ASSUMED that everyone lived in a world of vibrating color, where walls of pink felt met purple tweed cushions on top of vermillion carpets and maroon-upholstered furniture.

Alas, they did not.

But we did.

My father, David Hicks, woke up the drawing rooms of England by mixing yesterday with today before anybody else did. Who else had thought to place a Louis XV commode in a modern room? It was the sort of confident design choice that blew away the cobwebs of staid thinking and safe choices. His rooms made a statement. You can tell a Hicks room when you see it.

I carry this legacy forward.

Though our rooms tend to be much airier after twenty-five years in the Bahamas, David, my husband, and I often juxtapose found objects with interesting furniture. In our Oxfordshire sitting room, my mother's extraordinary set of Napoleonic bergères covered in fabric by Father and a majestic Georgian mirror and console could feel overly serious. But it's my mother's swimming caps encased in Perspex as a sort of Pop Art topiary that stand out in a room full of treasures.

If you haven't spent time in rooms that are a mad mix of modern and traditional, you might talk yourself out of buying something wonderful just because you think it won't work in your space. Nonsense. It can absolutely work. Thank God Paloma wrote this book. She'll show you how and give you peeks into some amazing homes where her design honors the architecture and gives the families more than they likely imagined when they bought or built the homes.

Paloma's modern take on traditional style is completely brilliant. She layers pieces of different eras and varying styles fearlessly and doesn't shy away from bold prints.

Flipping through this gorgeous book will help anyone who wants to learn to mix modern into the traditional absorb what that looks like when done well. But reading the stories of the homes, the care with which every detail was selected, and the joy that this dynamo of a woman brings to everything she does—that's the real treat.

OPPOSITE
Whether parading down a shelf or set in a tidy stack, the books of your home library create an ideal juxtaposition for collected art and sculptural objet. Shown here: our own Houston home, which I fell for in part for its abundant built-in shelving (I'm a bibliophile).

OPPOSITE
The DeGournay wall covering we selected for my client's Palm Beach home almost appears to burst forth from the walls, thanks to its metallic surface and the leafy fern in the foreground. *Big Bloom* peony photograph by Paul Lange.

WHEN I PUBLISHED MY FIRST BOOK, *Dream Design Live,* in 2018, my goal was to share some of my favorite things that I had learned for setting the foundation of design. From figuring out your "visual DNA" or personal aesthetic, to laying the groundwork for the steps you can take, it was filled with actionable advice and tutorials for all of the practical elements of designing a home. I am grateful that my career has evolved significantly over these past several years, affording me the opportunity to design amazing homes for the loveliest people in truly beautiful places. When I set out to write my second book, I knew I wanted to reflect on what makes for truly special and magical interiors. My goal is to share a bit of that magic with you.

My design sensibility is a modern take on traditional style. I tend to lean toward classic silhouettes and timeless pieces paired with a touch of glamour and an infusion of color. As much as I love Louis XVI furniture, chinoiserie wallpaper, and skirted upholstery, I am just as mad about Saarinen tulip tables, abstract contemporary art, and a sexy 1970s French aesthetic. Would mixing these elements result in a dizzying clash of aesthetics? How does one bridge the gap between such different concepts? I am here to show you the many ways in which traditional pieces can work seamlessly with modern ones. In fact, I firmly believe that the most interesting and successful interiors are those that feature elements from different eras and different styles. They tend to be more timeless, as they are inherently more layered, and I believe they're more personal than spaces that have furnishings from a single style or period.

LEFT A pair of sleek Lucite and brass martini tables contrast perfectly against this sumptuously tufted and bullion fringed settee in my client's Palm Beach foyer.

OPPOSITE Black and white art pieces always play well together, and can set off gold-gilt frames and other metallics as beautifully as cuff links on a tuxedo.

In *The New Classic Home*, we will explore the many ways in which I successfully pair seemingly disparate pieces from different eras and of varying styles to create harmonious, timeless, and balanced interiors. I will show you how I incorporate antiques and vintage pieces into even the most contemporary settings. We will touch on some of my favorite elements that work in any architectural style, as well as how to add a bit of tension to create nuanced, interesting spaces that include an element of surprise. Tension is a critical element in any space and one of my most favorite to introduce into a room. It is what takes a room from good to great and what can make a home truly sing! Creating a sense of juxtaposition infuses a space with character. After all, a sense of the unexpected makes everything more exciting—including one's home. You will find that there are many ways of implementing this magic mix—the ratio is truly personal to your home and your own aesthetic.

This time around, the book is organized by project. You'll find homes that run the gamut in terms of style, from a classic and feminine home in Houston, to a glamorous tropical house in Palm Beach, to a chic coastal home on the Jersey Shore, and everything in between! I have even included the new iteration of my own home, which you'll see has changed quite a bit since my first book. While each of these projects is tailored to the locale, architecture, and spirit of my client's individual home, my hope is that you will find the common thread connecting them. They all have their own special mix of modern and traditional elements that make them truly unique to the families who live in these wonderful houses. ✳

RIGHT If you have even a glimmer of an ocean view, take full advantage. In my client's New Jersey vacation home, that meant installing a nod to nautical in the form of softly striped sea blue wall covering in the third-floor primary suite. Unexpected details—a scalloped tray here, modern art there—keep it looking fresh.

WELCOME HOME

THE MAGIC IS IN THE MIX

OPPOSITE Mixing eras and provenances is key to a collected look. In our Houston dining room, I surrounded a table I ordered from Bunny Williams Home with 1930s-era dining chairs created in Paris by architect and designer André Arbus, a member of Académie des Beaux-Arts.

FINDING A NEW HOME IS NEVER EASY, especially in today's dizzying real estate market. You can be smitten with a perfect-looking listing on Zillow, then show up to discover that it's actually a fixer-upper of epic proportions. My advice is to seek out a property that already has some of the more vital bones in place—such as a functional layout, abundant daylight, and beautiful woodwork—and then make it your own.

When my husband and I decided to make an offer on this contemporary brick home in Houston's Museum District, one of the things that sold us on the place was the living room. We instantly fell in love with its large black steel windows that get incredible light throughout the day, and the massive built-in bookshelves that flank one wall. I had amassed an extensive coffee table book collection that I needed room for, so that existing storage was a big selling point. We also adored the layout and some of the foundational elements, such as tall ten-foot ceilings and millwork and moldings that gave it character.

Still, unless you build your own home from the ground up, you will probably want to make tweaks. This house—which we recently moved out of—was no exception, and we gave it a good facelift. We didn't move walls or alter the floor plan, yet no surface went untouched. Out went the previous owner's buttery yellow paint colors, granite counters, and clunky light fixtures . . . and in went choices that felt more like us.

I always think of lighting as the jewelry of the home. And while some may consider it a finishing touch, I find it to be fundamental to the overall mood of a room. It can add a glamorous flair or even provide a note of contrast in a space. To that end, I often prefer to layer in the lighting once I've outfitted the furniture. If we choose traditional seating choices, I can select a cool modern light fixture or lamp. I never want a space to feel like it's all one note, and lighting is a wonderful way to achieve a space that feels complex and compelling, with loads of personality. And just like the glimmering baubles in your jewelry box, great lighting is well worth a splurge. Allocate a healthy part of your design budget to it, because fixtures that are cheap or not the right scale can easily mar an otherwise lovely interior.

For our baby daughter Margot's nursery, I selected a shallow ceiling light in a silhouette that felt French. I am an unabashed Francophile and set out to design her room knowing that I wanted to create a space that felt magical, and that would stir her imagination. Children's rooms should have a sense of longevity, so opt for selections you find timeless. I kicked off the color palette with a fanciful yet enduring choice—a chinoiserie wallpaper with pink hues and varying shades of green that is dotted with flora and fauna. I just loved all the transportive flowers and birds and felt that as Margot got older, she would have a lot to take in and dream about. I often caught her smiling at its peacocks and butterflies . . . which made me smile, too. Oftentimes she would point to the birds while I rocked her to sleep, which is sure to become a treasured memory as she grows older. Above the crib, I hung a crisp photograph of the Jardin des Tuileries in Paris. It adds a fresh element to a room anchored by a centuries-old wallpaper design and creates a nice tension between the modern and traditional. Because I firmly believe it is important to remember the fifth wall, or the

ceiling, I painted Margot's a soft, faint-as-a-whisper pink. It complements the colors in the wallpaper without being expected and looks dreamy overhead.

In our own bedroom, I cozied up the soaring tray ceiling by sheathing the walls in moiré wall covering in a mocha hue. I've been obsessed with moiré for ages, because it reminds me of glamorous vintage dresses from the 1940s and '50s. When we hung this wallpaper, it immediately transformed the room to feel rich, warm, and inviting. It catches the light nicely in the daytime, and after dusk gives off this delicious chocolate tone. Atop that creamy foundation, I layered a few of my trademarks: abstract art, ikat fabrics, bamboo details, and even a crusty Louis XVI gilt bench for good measure. The symmetrical placement is easier for the eye to process and feels more balanced, which is restful in a bedroom.

Of course, every home needs central gathering spaces that feel welcoming and reflect the owner's personality. In our dining room, I swapped the ornate panels we originally hung on the wall for nine graphic abstract works by a southern artist named Jane Timberlake Cooper, out of Birmingham. They're wonderfully textural—made of plaster, charcoal, and string on Japanese paper that's been glossed over—a nod to the late Cy Twombly. Hung in a tidy grid of nine, they have the visual impact of one oversized piece. Juxtaposed against them, chairs made in 1930s Paris by André Arbus and a glimmering chandelier strike a graceful note.

One thing I really love to do is to style shelves, which you'll see in our former living room. I've become known for it—by association or osmosis—and enjoy tackling the task in clients' homes and in our store as well. For me, the most important thing is that bookshelves hold actual books—preferably meaningful tomes you know and love. To keep my own book collections from looking too heavy or uninteresting, I mix in different objects, such as French pottery and art. (As a card-carrying magpie, I'm drawn to anything sparkly and shiny.) You'll notice the books are arranged in different ways—some vertical,

OPPOSITE Our tawny-hued cockapoo, Tate, perfectly matches this Louis XVI chest I found in France. The graphic nero marquina marble slab on top is new—marrying something modern with traditional—and the rest is original, down to the hardware (an uncommon find). The art piece above is by New Orleans painter Alexis Walter.

some horizontal—which provides variation for the eye. Underneath the shelving, cabinets tucked away Margot's playthings and her own burgeoning library of children's books.

At every seat, there is always a table nearby to hold a book or a cocktail. That's something I learned from Bunny Williams many years ago. She said she always makes sure that regardless of where you roost, there is a spot to set your stuff on. That's the true mark of a functional room: It's always accommodating, even if all you need is a place to rest your martini while you dance. ✳

LEFT A few years ago, I had our living room's white sofas reupholstered in a moss green velvet (I was longing to move in a more traditional direction, and the change had enormous impact!). In black, the coffee table I custom-designed lends gravitas to the space, with a cane top to lighten the mood a bit. We live casually, but I couldn't help but increase the room's glamour with a Georgian giltwood mirror I found at auction. It's overscaled and suits the 10-foot-high ceilings perfectly.

LEFT There is no space that can't be made more charming and timeless with the addition of topiaries. Paired with a stone sculpture, they pop alongside modern art pieces and a graphic brass lamp from my collection.

OPPOSITE The occasional animal print (such as a leopard-print throw pillow) and polished brass vase supply instant liveliness to any interior.

CY TWOMBLY GALLERY

AD at 100

RIGHT Nesting is such a joyful process, especially when you live and breathe design. For our daughter Margot's nursery, I wanted to welcome her to the world by surrounding her with nods to the incredible beauty found in nature (like the peacock dancing across her Iksel chinoiserie wallpaper) and cities (such as the Jardin des Tuileries in Paris hung above her crib). I bought the bow chair as soon as I found out I was pregnant with a girl, and it has quickly become one of her favorites.

LEFT Everyone—at any age—can appreciate a good fabric. Margot and I love cuddling up in this velvet gilder for storytime; books are very important for fostering imagination. Note that we painted the ceiling of her nursery a soft pink—it casts a beautiful, warm glow.

OPPOSITE We carry Ornis Gallery prints in my shop, Paloma & Co, and I loved this eighteenth-century Swedish swan for the spot above the changing table. While it's a water bird, it's still appropriate with the wallpaper. The table is a simple Ikea piece dressed up with solid brass hardware that's worth more than the dresser itself—talk about high and low!

LEFT Our formerly gray primary bedroom has transformed a lot over the years. This latest iteration proved to me how a few relatively simple tweaks—such as hanging silk moiré wall covering from Schumacher in a rich cocoa brown and a light fixture from my own collection for Visual Comfort—can lead to an incredible transformation. The chocolate details on our bedding pull it all together.

HOW THEY DECORATED P. Gaye Tapp

Michael S Smith The Curated House

from CLASSIC to CONTEMPORARY ELISSA CULLMAN AND TRACEY PRUZAN

OPPOSITE You can really get a sense for why I'm obsessed with silk moiré wallpaper in this vignette: It's a sumptuous backdrop for everything from traditional bamboo pieces to modern art, and its motion is as transfixing as the waves of the sea. The light is my own Orsay Medium Table Lamp, designed for Visual Comfort.

RIGHT Personalizing your bedding with monograms and a color that's tailored to your tastes is one of the best ways to set a dreamy tone you'll love coming home to for years to come.

RIGHT The over-sized iron windows in our dining room flood the space with light and give the house so much character. We recently swapped a triptych of De Gournay panels with nine abstract works by Jane Timberlake Cooper, and our old Louis XVI dining chairs with more modern 1930s André Arbus seats. The metamorphosis was instant and—as Arbus himself might say—*incroyable*.

EN FAMILLE

WHERE FAMILY-FRIENDLY
MEETS FABULOUS

OPPOSITE We brought a fresh yet traditional feeling into this Austin, Texas, family of three's modern farmhouse with storied details (a scroll arm here, a drapery trim there) in a palette of cool blues and natural hues.

SOMETIMES, THE WORD *childproof* can elicit a groan among the world's design cognoscenti. They may worry it translates to primary colors and a bit too much washable vinyl. But believe me, it's possible to create pretty—no, downright *sumptuous* interiors that are both timeless and able to take some wear and tear (and plenty of spills!) from residents of all ages. For proof, look no further than this home I designed for clients in Austin, Texas. They are the sweetest family with three young children—and, by some miracle, the owners of a completely pristine house.

For their modern farmhouse–style abode, we took a traditional approach but freshened it up just a bit, with layers of cool blue and green hues. Because these clients moved to Texas to be closer to their extended family during the COVID-19 pandemic, they had been living in the home for a while with little to no furniture. As such, their directive was clear: They wanted it to feel very cozy and inviting. They're lovely, casual people, but longed for a house that was tailored and beautiful.

Although nothing in the home is off limits to their children, we made a few choices to help keep their pretty palace pretty spotless. First, we created a playroom in the game room upstairs that's a major draw—so the kids sprawl out with their toys there, and not in the photo-ready main living spaces. We also had nearly every furniture piece treated by Fiber-Seal, a service that arrives at your door to make upholstery fabric stain resistant. We cheekily call it our "sleep-at-night factor"! It's a bit of extra protection to safeguard your investment from children, pets, or the party guest who tipsily spills their Merlot right on your cream-colored sofa. Any mishaps will just sit on the fabric's surface, like raindrops on glass, until they're dabbed away. Say it with me: *phew*.

We also almost always choose performance fabrics for our upholstery. For the sofas in this home, we selected a beautiful cotton velvet that happened to be performance rated. The breakfast nook also has performance fabrics—many designed by smaller boutique fabric designers and makers, like Peter Dunham. It's quite a departure from a few years ago, when every "performance" fabric felt like a striped outdoor cabana cushion!

One trick to embracing beauty in a home with little ones is to indulge in incredible art. You can often hang it safely out of reach of little fingers, or at the very least bolt it quite securely to the wall—and it provides so much to delight the eye. Here in the breakfast nook, we installed a piece by fine-art photographer Dale Goffigon. Art is one of those things that I'm flexible on, because it's so subjective. It really has to evoke something for the homeowners, because it's so personal! Even if I think something's perfect, if they don't love it, we keep looking. I sent them a few select pieces by this particular photographer to consider, and they adored this one the moment they saw it. If you need to add art that feels a bit more modern, photography generally reads fresh and graphic in a space. We all loved that it's green and lush like the surrounding accessories, and it seems to beckon the viewer into the scene. Placing it above the breakfast nook's bench also felt like it added more architecture to the room. In the dining room, a piece by Alexis Walter has the scrawled effect of an unfettered child's artwork, while nodding to the tonal color palette of Monet's *Water Lilies* series. (Tip: Placing a painting you

RIGHT In the living room, I selected a substantially sized coffee table whose clipped corners buy you a bit of real estate (and are child-friendly). Its muted grasscloth finish adds additional texture to the room. The acrylic book holder is something I sell in my shop, Paloma & Co, and a perfect inspiration to regularly revamp your trove of tomes on display.

love across from a mirror effectively doubles your view and your enjoyment of it.)

Certainly every parent deserves a retreat for for some well-earned R&R. For these clients' primary bedroom, we created an indulgent cocoon around their existing bed, including appliqué bedding with a monogram and Greek key details. A bamboo trim on the leading edge of the drapery, an acrylic curtain rod, and curvaceous, textural raffia bedside chests helped whip up a veritable self-care hideaway. We spend so much time decorating our children's nurseries, but remember, when you're a new parent, you're being reborn in a way, too. Treat yourself! ✳

OPPOSITE When the mantel is buttoned-up and traditional, like this marble and herringbone tile version, I often can't help but hang a modern art piece with lots of movement above it.

LEFT Maidenhair ferns are notoriously divas, but all the struggle to keep them happy—including near-constant misting—is well worth it, because they're as delicate and enthralling as lace..

LEFT Graphic throw pillows bring levity to a pattern-less sofa. I've always loved pairing ikat with a Greek key—an ancient pattern that's been found in Byzantine, Etruscan, and Roman architecture as well, and was reportedly inspired by the snaking loops of the Turkish Maeander River.

OPPOSITE We wanted all the rooms in this home to speak to one another, flowing naturally from one to the next. For this formerly all-white bathroom, we painted the existing vanity a deep Yale blue. Adding a sweet dose of prettiness above: plaster sconces with leaf details, wallpaper by Alex Conroy, and a mirror inspired by a midcentury Italian version.

OPPOSITE
Because they are a
young family, it was
important for this
dining nook where
they eat the major-
ity of their meals at
home to feel youth-
ful and timeless. I
brought in a French
ticking stripe for
the seat upholstery,
and the lushness of
Peter Dunham's fig
leaf fabric on throw
pillows. The mix of
casual materials is
very inviting.

RIGHT Layering
and textures are
essential for a beau-
tiful tablescape.
Here, we dotted
the surface with
cut hydrangea and
myrtle topiaries
and used multiple
patterns—ranging
from bubbled
glass tumblers to
marbled plates—to
delight the eye. The
Poppy tablecloth
is from my shop,
Paloma & Co.

LEFT Robin's egg blue walls in the dining room differentiate it from the more casual spaces in the home. We paired a modern oval dining table in cerused oak with classic Louis XVI dining chairs with a square back. (If I had a toolbox of design elements I could use again and again for the rest of my career, the latter would be in there, because they look fabulous with any style of table you can imagine!)

OPPOSITE The hand-painted lines of this gourd lamp have a child-like quality that's restful to the eye in the bedroom, especially when set alongside an earthy vase of fresh-cut garden blooms.

RIGHT The clients kept their existing blue velvet bed for the primary suite, and we brought in pretty appliqué bedding with a monogram and Greek key details, plus curved night-stands wrapped in a textural raffia. Lucite pulls and drapery rods bring in the glamour. It's a very relaxed home, so adding that material gives a little wink to the spaces.

LEFT For the primary bathroom's vanity, we selected new sconces and a mirror edged in antiqued Greek key details. I love to monogram towels in the bathroom, too—it makes it feel like your own personal spa.

OPPOSITE We added a lot of softness to this room. You can't go wrong with Carrara marble, simple white cabinetry, and brushed nickel fixtures, but we did warm up the utilitarian space with custom Roman shades to match the motif in the primary suite. The Oushak rug by the tub supplies a bit of color underfoot.

SECRET GARDENS

THE JOYS OF BRINGING
THE OUTDOORS IN

OPPOSITE
By nature, pocket doors are meant to slip away—but that doesn't mean they can't stand out. For this Houston home, we thought it would be really fun to also wallpaper the pocket doors separating this dining room from the more utilitarian butler's pantry in the same incredible Schumacher chinoiserie.

THE MOST SHOWSTOPPING GARDENS in the world have a few things in common: lush, manicured grounds with nary a leaf out of place; abundant blossoms; and a bit of architecture for all the wild wonders of nature to be juxtaposed against. They're as inherently calming and refreshing as a walk through the morning dew.

It's possible to bring the emotional feeling of these exquisite gardens—of strolling through the ornamental boxwoods of France's Château de Villandry on a June morning, for example—into your own house. We did just that in this Houston home, which is owned by a couple I've been friends with since high school! Designing a home is a very long process, and it was fun to have such an established history with these fantastic clients.

Sometimes, the real estate gods work in mysterious ways. When a golf community property they'd been working toward fell through, they realized how much they love their current neighborhood—and decided to stay put. We did an extensive renovation on their 1960s house, dreaming up the perfect interiors that would be tailored just for them and their two teenage kids. We gutted the former kitchen and added a butler's pantry along with a fanciful and airy mudroom, sheathed in hand-hewn zellige tile.

The adjacent dining room really does resurrect the feeling of wandering a French estate. We lined the entire space in a Schumacher chinoiserie wall covering, including the pocket doors—a fun, surprising element that, when closed, totally envelops you in the room. We were drawn to this specific paper for its pretty greens with hints of blue and even pale pink, which felt so fresh. White oak floors underfoot keep the aesthetic light and earthy.

In the kitchen, marble wall tiles, a deep farm sink, and multiple topiaries add to the luxuriant garden feel. This couple may not be big home cooks, but they couldn't help treating themselves to a La Cornue stove. They've been made in France since 1908 and are jewelry for your kitchen, worth the investment. In this open floor plan, the stove instantly became a riveting focal point—especially in timeless stainless steel and unlacquered brass. When you glance from there out the windows, you take in a gorgeous overlook of their gardens, with a parade of jasmine blossoms.

Each member of a family often finds a favorite spot to call their own in every home. Here, the husband's favorite space is undoubtedly a hunter green hideaway he calls his Bourbon Room. He is to bourbon whiskey what oenophiles are to wine, and he collects bourbon from all around the globe. (Proof he's obsessed: He hosts a podcast about spirits and records it right there in the room!) We painted the space Benjamin Moore Cushing Green, partly inspired by the Polo Bar in New York City, but added plenty of mirrors to bounce light from the terrace and pool back into the space so it never feels dark. The reflection of the gardens from them is quite lovely; just another way to bring the best of the outdoors in. ✳

RIGHT The butler's pantry is almost another full working kitchen (convenient, since it's right off the dining room), complete with a microwave, refrigerator, wine fridge, and plenty of dry storage for tabletop treasures like stemware and linens.

OPPOSITE This handmade Moroccan Zellige tile on the backsplash has a lot of movement to it, because each piece is made individually. They don't sit perfectly flush against the wall the way a machine-made tile would, which is part of what makes them so beautiful—I love the subtle variation from each one to the next.

LEFT The home-owner really wanted chinoiserie for her dining room, and we were instantly drawn to the color palette in this particular paper—designed by Miles Redd for Schumacher—with its soft greens, hints of blues, and even the occasional pink. It felt so fresh, like a spring day! We custom-made the host and hostess chairs as a lovely juxtaposition against the Ballard side chairs. It feels more personal and dynamic that way, and less like a set.

OPPOSITE Be sure to vary the heights of the "skyline" on your tabletop to create interest. Here, we used brass candlesticks and flower arrangements at various levels as a centerpiece—it's often a more satisfying setup than one simple bouquet or a candelabra.

RIGHT To work with the existing pedestal sink in this powder room, we brought in a new faucet, mirror, and drippy sconces and that fun wallpaper, which really envelops you and draws you in with its movement. It's pretty and whimsical, yet doesn't take away from the chinoiserie in the dining room.

LEFT We completed a full gut renovation of this kitchen. The focal point in the open space is undoubtedly the La Cornue stove: With its combination of stainless steel and unlacquered brass finishes, it's the definition of timeless. Above the island, the airy fixture allows the daylight to flow without taking up too much visual real estate. Woven stools supply a casual, warm texture.

FOLLOWING What could possibly work well with such an elegant stove? As with any delicious recipe, you need to lean in to appropriate pairings. Here, that meant a marble tile backsplash soaring to the ceiling and brass detailing (including on the range hood). The farmhouse sink will never go out of style . . . ditto roman shades, especially with a custom Greek key trim.

RIGHT To lighten up the living room, we added this entire wall of French doors. This is the hub of the house and basically the center of their universe, so great light was key! I wanted to create a space that was casual yet tailored and polished, and this blue and white color palette delivered. Because sectionals aren't the most exciting things in the world, I surrounded this one with interesting tables, including an acrylic one and a lacquered one with curved legs. We also added the exposed beams overhead—they give the architecture a bit of rhythm.

LEFT Practical and highly functional rooms can still be beauties, as this mudroom will attest. Set off the home's back entrance, it's a main thoroughfare, so needed to stand up to frequent use. We selected a hard-wearing performance fabric for the bench cushion and tucked lots of concealed storage everywhere (including easy-to-grab-from woven baskets).

OPPOSITE For the pool bath off the mudroom, I felt everything should be fresh and fun. I chose a geometrically patterned wallcovering and mixed the metals of the lighting and faucet. With its brass accents, the Art Deco mirror bridges the gap between the two.

ABOVE Anytime you want to make a space feel more personal, add a monogram. These pillows are embroidered with a monogram on the larger side—my go-to when I want something to have a more graphic quality. Otherwise, this is a very soft and traditional space, with symmetrical styling that feels very restful to the eye.

OPPOSITE White grosgrain tape trim creates a border on both the seat and the back cushion of this Dutch blue settee. When the view out the window is of a beautifully manicured garden, I often can't help but bring its lushness indoors a bit (here: a pair of garden stools-turned-side tables and ball topiaries).

OPPOSITE Placing sconces directly on a mirror effectively doubles the light they give off. Tiny touches in this bathroom, including blue and white chinoiserie porcelain pieces and woven scalloped trays, make it a wonderful room to linger in while prepping for the day.

LEFT I often place a diminutive cocktail table next to a soaking tub, especially in a primary bathroom. They're the perfect place to rest everything from toiletries to your latest beach read, and so easy to move around.

LEFT The home-owner collects bourbon from all over the globe, so he has appropriately deemed this his Bourbon Room. He even records his podcast here! To switch it up from the blues of the main living areas, we settled on this studious green hue inspired by the Polo Bar and took it from the floor to the ceiling. The mirrored backsplash helps reflect the light from the pool and garden.

OPPOSITE He loves his collection of black-and-white prints from the series *Lonesome Dove*, so we embraced it. The abstract piece is country singer George Strait—always a joyful sight to raise your glass to.

FLORIDA FANTASY

FANCIFYING TRADITIONS

ONE OF THE BEST PARTS of being a designer is the wonderful people you meet. This client stumbled across my first book in a boutique at Key Largo's Ocean Reef Club, where she and her husband have one of their homes. When they decided to buy another place in Palm Beach, she reached out to hire me—and I'm beyond thrilled that she did. We are very simpatico, with similar aesthetic tastes. We nearly finish each other's sentences!

When this couple first purchased the West Indies–style property, they longed for it to feel coastal and tropical. It needed a light refresh to live up to the Palm Beach aesthetic of their dreams. The home had great curb appeal and really good bones, but they longed to make it feel like their own. We made mindful changes to the materials and layout of the house to make it more conducive to the way my client and her family utilize the spaces and to reflect her personal style. The home's existing interiors were surprisingly dark, with wood surfaces and dark materials practically everywhere the eye could see. Eventually, they brought on an architect, and over the course of a year, we undertook a gut renovation that included adding a new primary suite.

We worked hand in hand with the architect to convey the spirit of the home and the design and finish elements that make it special. And it *is* special, down to the tiniest detail. We gave it the effortless style that you want in a vacation home by the water, but it's a little bit more glamorous—thanks to formal and unexpected moments that are distinctive, though not stuffy by

OPPOSITE My clients' Palm Beach home had the exterior vernacular of West Indies-style architecture. We transformed it quite a bit: It feels like a brand-new house. One key approach: increasing the focus on indoor/outdoor living by swapping in more French doors for existing smaller windows.

any means. One of the bones of contention during our standing weekly meetings with our client, architect, and builder was the staircase. The architect originally suggested a quintessential Chinese Chippendale railing, but our client felt it would be too predictable, especially in this town. "I don't want this house to be the typical Palm Beach house . . . I want it to be a little different," she said. To come up with something extraordinary, I did a lot of research and spent many late nights poring over historical architectural plans. We ended up finding another Chippendale design that dates to a seventeenth-century British manor home, the Chinese star motif. The architect worked tirelessly to scale it perfectly for a railing, and the builder was wonderful in getting it executed.

Another "wow" moment comes in the form of the exultant wall covering in the great room. From the second I set foot in that space, I knew it would be amazing to do an incredible hand-painted wallpaper. For that, I almost always have three syllables to utter to my clients: *de Gournay*. There's something about de Gournay papers that feels a little bit more fresh and modern than the alternatives. Some of that has to do with the way the company spaces its designs; it intentionally builds in negative space so they're not as dense, which gives the intricacy of the motifs room to breathe.

We chose a tropical wallpaper very much in keeping with Palm Beach style, yet not cliché in any way. Because we had added French doors to the space, we selected a silver metallic background for the wall covering to bounce even more natural light around. We were able to temper the formality of the paper with casual elements, such as white slipcovered sofas, rattan chairs, and a jute rug. That allowed us to lean in hard to glamorous and feminine silk shantung drapery treatments. In an expansive room like this, with its ten-foot ceilings, curtains as full as a ball gown really dazzle.

Honestly, there was not one inch of this house we didn't get to touch and make into something truly beautiful—in part because these clients gave me full creative license. Even the elevator got an upgrade! The husband uses it every day, and since he's a navy alum and has done a ton for the U.S. Armed Forces, we honored him by dressing it in blue and white, sheathing the interior in Pierre Frey's Toile de Nantes wallpaper, and even having a railing custom-made from Lucite with brass accents.

Speaking of unexpected: One of the dreamiest moments we designed is in the foyer, where you'll see a little seating area tucked under the stairs. The previous owners kept a pair of fountains in enormous urns there, which we quickly relieved of their duty. Instead, we opted to make an intimate, cozy spot for tête-à-têtes. When I first mentioned the idea to my client, I said, "Just imagine how fabulous it would be to cozy up for a private conversation in that spot in the midst of a bustling party." Sitting there, you can practically hear the ghosts of Palm Beach past giggling into the wee hours. While the house is a glamorous respite in an iconic town, the best compliment has come from my client, who says it truly feels like home. ✳

OPPOSITE West Indies–style architecture was created in the eighteenth and nineteenth centuries by the British in the Caribbean Islands. Some of its hallmarks include stucco walls, the Palladian proportions endemic to Georgian-era homes, and—as you'll note here—plenty of symmetry.

LEFT I'm a firm believer in the power of details. Like the stair rail we designed that echoed one in a seventeenth-century British estate, the exceedingly wide doorway portal here is adorned in a motif that echoes flouncy palm tree fronds created by the architect. It's one of the things that make the house truly special. In the blank space under the stairs, we took the opportunity to create a moment with a cozy banquette dressed to the Palm Beach nines in velvet and fringe.

OPPOSITE Intricate shellwork was beloved during the Italian Renaissance, and it suits this impromptu sitting area in the foyer beautifully in the form of a showstopping mirror crafted by hand using abalone shells. We balanced its maximalist look with a comparatively streamlined chest and chairs.

RIGHT I knew we needed to do something quite special in the combination living and dining room, because it's a huge part of the house: You navigate it to reach the kitchen and family room. The de Gournay wallpaper we selected strikes a good balance between the care-free feeling of living by the sea and the more buttoned-up, gala-ready side of Palm Beach.

LEFT While the great room would be the most formal space in the house, it still needed to be somewhat casual and inviting. The happy green silk shantung draperies help with that. We pulled their color right from the wallpaper. As you can see, I like my draperies full—especially in a large room with a lofty ceiling.

OPPOSITE We brought the lush tropical garden right to the tabletop with a bevy of pink, orange, and white florals and even cut fruit for decor. Joyful, tactile pieces—such as polka-dotted tumblers, scalloped placemats, and fringed coral napkins have the same jovial feeling as a stroll on the shore.

RIGHT The rattan chairs, white slip-covered sofas, and abaca rug bring a necessary casual feeling to this otherwise formal affair of a room. A little modernity, too, was key, such as our custom-designed lacquer and brass coffee table.

FOLLOWING No detail is too small to fuss over until it feels just right. When in doubt, go for something custom or rarely seen . . . the final effect will transfix every guest and make your home feel like your very own.

LEFT One thing that really stands out about this kitchen is that it has incredible views of the garden on all sides. Our client wanted to maximize that and feel like she was al fresco whenever she stepped foot in the cookspace. To achieve that, we limited upper cabinetry and limited the color palette to put the focus on all the lush greens beyond the windows.

OPPOSITE We selected clean-lined inset cabinetry with unlacquered brass hardware, and a very rare slab of Calacatta Gold Borghini Diamond marble for the counters with soft veining she fell in love with. She's very wellness-oriented, so we tucked a lot of refrigerator drawers in this cookspace to keep produce as fresh and nutrient-dense as possible.

RIGHT Hidden behind a jib door in the kitchen, this sweet pantry feels ultra-special thanks to an iconic wallpaper: Brunschwig & Fils Les Touches, introduced in 1965. No space in this home, no matter how utilitarian, went untouched! I love how the sleek floating shelves make it pack an even more powerful punch.

LEFT This living space just off the pool is where my clients spend the most time when they're here, so we made sure everything you'd need was on hand—including a fabulous bar. I often layer lighting in spaces, such as the combination of ceiling pendants and sconces. The fixtures cast a warm and welcoming glow for cocktail hour, ensuring the mood is just right.

OPPOSITE A waterfall-edge island is all the more luxe and timeless-looking when you opt for an extra-thick mitered edge. We softened the visual heaviness of this with the woven McGuire bar stools and intricate ceiling and bar details.

LEFT A glass NanaWall opens completely to the terrace and pool, which is an ideal feature during Palm Beach's near-perfect winters. We opted for different shades of blue and white here to echo the water and sky. The customized hexagonal ottoman has an inset cerused oak tray that you can pull out for serving.

RIGHT All the stone we used outside was coquina, or coral stone, as it is commonly known. It is native to Florida and helps give this home a true sense of place. To ensure that your outdoor spaces are just as beloved as the indoor ones, keep comfort top of mind. You'll want to include all the things you love and need inside, including plush seating options and multiple sources of light for a flattering glow after dusk.

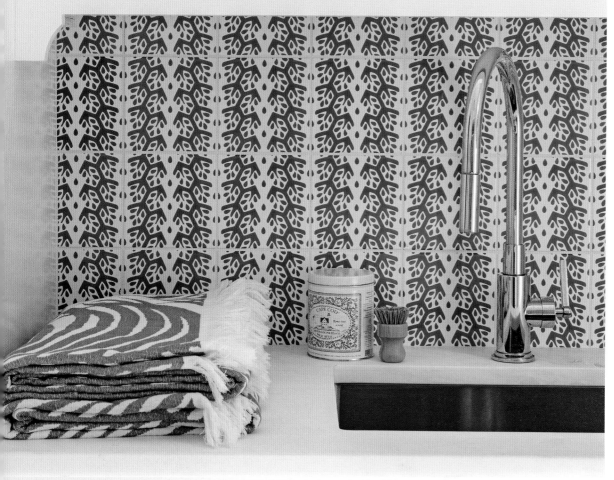

LEFT The blue and white touches we installed throughout the property aren't just beachy or a classic, tried-and-true pairing. They're a reverent and grateful nod to the homeowner, a navy alum.

OPPOSITE In limiting the color palette in the alfresco areas, we gave nature the floor. Against neutral whites and sandy hues, the verdant greens in thick hedges and blush pinks on the climbing bougainvillea take center stage.

OPPOSITE Even in an interior hallway, you can bring a taste for the outdoors to the space. Here, we focused on a textural wall covering with a flora pattern and a pendant light with trellis and palm tree-inspired details. Ultra-high crown molding lends the passageway a historic feel.

RIGHT Maya Romanoff's Mother of Pearl Oyster shell wallpaper is as lustrous and luminous as it looks and installed in 12 × 12-inch tiles. My client is from Oyster Bay, New York, so absolutely loved it paired with the oyster shell mirror in this powder room.

RIGHT For the primary bedroom, we opted for a gleaming Paul Ferrante bed that looks like a modern version of bamboo. She asked for Palm Beach colors here, but rather than doing a bright coral, we selected a more serene hue that mimics the inside of a seashell. Keeping the lines very crisp prevented it from reading as overly feminine.

FOLLOWING Letting draperies puddle a bit at the floor is vital for a luxurious feel. I also love using a duvet cover with a border: It helps define the bed within the space. The painting is by New Orleans-based artist Alexis Walter. To my eye, the colors in it felt perfect: different from the rest of the room without veering too far from the initial intent.

OPPOSITE The feeling of a private home spa in the primary bath is much coveted by clients these days. This couple has the ultimate setup: a full primary bath for her, and a separate full primary bath for him. Hers is particularly sumptuous, with a deep soaking tub and walk-in shower.

RIGHT We used very pretty miniature square mosaic mother-of-pearl tiles behind the vanity in her bathroom, which adds texture to the space and brings in the seashell motif without being obvious. Lush foliage beyond her window and the mirror's central placement help keep the feeling private.

LEFT I advise every one of my clients to meet me in the showroom and actually get into the soaking tub they're interested in before deciding on the purchase. As with a sofa, you'll want to ensure it suits your frame and will be comfortable. It's vital, because once a tub is installed, it's not exactly easy to swap out! This one is perfect for a long, relaxing bath.

OPPOSITE Before we added a new primary suite in the remodel, this guest room was the primary. We wallpapered it in an iconic pattern I've always adored—Quadrille's China Seas Lyford Trellis—which helps the space embrace a truly tropical vibe. I kept the rest of the room crisp and clean to not overwhelm the space.

RIGHT Florida is home to myriad native orchid species—106 of them, at last count, including the Florida butterfly orchid and rare ghost orchid (famous for its role in Susan Orlean's book *The Orchid Thief*). So of course, I couldn't help but take them as muse!

OPPOSITE We clad the room her daughter uses when she visits in grasscloth: a fantastic, textural touch that cozies up any space. Using the same Quadrille fabric on the curtains and throw pillow on the rattan chair creates a seamless look that's both luscious and easy to live with.

RIGHT The thick rug underfoot was woven from abaca—a sustainable fiber made from the leaves of a tropical plant that's related to the banana species. We selected it in part to vary the types of texture within this space, which helps keep things interesting for the eye.

LADIES FIRST

CREATE A PRIVATE STUDY
THAT LIVES LARGE

OPPOSITE For this showhouse in a double-width Georgian town house on East 74th Street in New York, we transformed a bedroom into a ladies' library. One of my muses for the color palette came from just beyond the windows: the fresh, vibrant buds and leaves of springtime bursting forth from the trees.

ONE OF THE BEST THINGS ABOUT participating in a designer showhouse is knowing that you have carte blanche over every single decision in the room. In addition to raising necessary funds for deserving charities, showhouses are a fabulous way to tap into your true design aesthetic and visual DNA without any sort of outside noise. I always look at projects like this as a challenge to tune into my heart's desire, and then execute it in a way that feels engaging. It's also vital to always retain a sense of place, reflecting the way people live in the showhouse's locale and speaking to that regional vernacular.

The 47th Annual Kips Bay Decorator Show House in Manhattan was tucked within an expansive double townhouse on the Upper East Side, and we were tasked with revamping a fourth-floor bedroom. I quickly decided to turn it into a lady's study. The space had beautiful original millwork and built-ins I wanted to preserve, and these gorgeous bay windows overlooking the leafy tree canopies of the street below.

This room is a representation of my true aesthetic at its core. Because there wasn't an actual real client, I imagined a dreamy one: a modern version of *Downton Abbey*'s Lady Mary, in her early twenties and embracing her career and social life full-throttle. Like many New Yorkers, she'd be obsessive about art, food, and culture. I pictured her inviting friends to her study for a nightcap after an evening at the Carlyle, just two blocks away.

To select this color palette, I pushed myself outside my usual bounds a little bit toward these very bold hues, looking to Valentino's most recent haute couture show for inspiration. Pierpaolo Piccioli had designed an exquisite array of sumptuous gowns in silk taffetas—all in bright, electrifying colors. That became my jumping-off point for the color palette in the room, and the reason I chose a silk moiré for the drapery. I liked that it felt like a dressmaker detail. It can't help but drip with glamour! It felt fresh and unexpected, yet classic.

A vibrant palette can be executed in a way that doesn't feel overwhelming if you purposefully choose mostly solid fabrics and paint the surrounding walls white. Here, that tactic not only served to highlight the pretty millwork that was original to the house, but also allowed the space to breathe a little bit. In a dark color or with tons of pattern, this same room would give off a completely different energy—and could feel a bit suffocating. The white in the room adds freshness and grounds it, much like the natural-fiber rug does. It prevents it from being too much.

In laying out the floor plan, I thought about functionality and what would feel gracious and practical but also intriguing (you have to put the *show* in *show house*!). I set up a little seating area where you could have a conversation or cocktail before going out, with a petite yet overstuffed settee in blue cotton velvet that's meant to be sumptuous and enveloping. Paired alongside it, the crisp white Napoleon-style barrel chairs with bullion fringe have a feminine silhouette and scale, but fit very comfortably. Ikat pillows made from vintage fabric bring all the colors in the room together perfectly.

Above the little writing desk—an actual period Louis XVI desk flanked by nineteenth-century Adams chairs—the red gathered shades on the sconces add a little pop that's unexpected. It's important to have something that feels like it doesn't belong 100 percent . . . otherwise, a space can feel overly decorated, rather than collected over

RIGHT We used a silver leaf wallpaper by Schumacher to complement the beautiful inlaid deGournay panels that we placed in the room's original millwork. A comparatively simple natural fiber rug and a few white furniture pieces keep the room a bit down to earth, allowing its more colorful characters to shine.

time. You can end up with a perfectly pretty room, but it might look like it was torn from the pages of a catalog instead of a real living, breathing space.

Throughout, art pieces—such as the abstracts by French painter Jacques Nestlé and contemporary Georgia artist Kimberly Moore—serve to add a bit of tension. For that same reason, every space needs a hint of black. It's not as intimidating as it sounds, because it can be something as small as a fringe detail, or a small drawing leaning in your bookshelf. It doesn't have to be one of the major pieces, but it can lend a gravitas and an elegance.

Because the study had gorgeous windows, I sheathed the ceiling in silver leaf to reflect the light. (It also complements the inlaid de Gournay panels we set within the millwork around the room.) Above the built-in bookcases, I hung eglomise mirrored panels to draw the eye up. They reflected that beautiful light and added another little touch of glam. In a town like New York, you can never have too much. ✳

OPPOSITE Every busy New Yorker needs a place to catch up on a little work at home—preferably one that looks nothing at all like a Midtown office. Who wouldn't enjoy sending emails from an authentic Louis XVI desk and nineteenth-century Adams chairs reupholstered in this happy cadmium yellow?

LEFT One of my favorite things about de Gournay wallpaper is how carefully it's made. The intricate motifs on the silk wall covering—inspired by historic versions found in European and Chinese estates—are painted by hand and can even be hand-embroidered with silk thread to add a more tactile touch.

LEFT The coffee table is an antique French piece by Maison Baguès—founded in 1860 Paris—with a pretty leaf detail on the legs and frame. I loved the mirrored top and the scale, which suits the sitting area perfectly. To prevent it from reading as stuffy or overly traditional, I placed handmade geometric plaster candlesticks by Stephen Antonson on the tabletop.

OPPOSITE Hints of pink, red, and coral in the de Gournay wallpaper inspired the sconces with gathered shades that fit within the millwork without coloring outside the lines. Don't forget the front of your bookshelves as a possible display spot for art: It really helps pieces pop.

DINING DELIGHT

SERVE UP A DINING ROOM
THAT WILL ALWAYS FEEL FRESH

OPPOSITE The sideboard in this dining room is a Louis XVI period piece I borrowed from an antiques dealer for the Lake Forest Designer Showhouse. Pairing it with equally traditional lighting could have easily felt stale, so I opted for a pair of vintage, midcentury-inspired brass lamps and topiaries that echo their shape.

IF JAY GATSBY HAD STAYED in his native Midwest to experience the Jazz Age in full *Great Gatsby* style, he might have ended up in Lake Forest. The hamlet due north of Chicago is chockablock with storied estates that are nothing short of cinematic. Take the twenty-three-room property that hosted a recent Lake Forest Designer Showhouse—designed in 1906 by Frost & Granger and revamped in 1929. It was exquisite, and something about the facade made it feel unimposing. It still felt like a cozy, welcoming house.

I was tasked with designing the dining room, a graciously scaled space that overlooked a verdant manicured garden. There were beautiful bones to work with and lots of amazing original details, such as the hardware on the doors and a built-in china cabinet, that were both incredibly charming and functional. Because my objective was to create something that felt appropriate for the place and time the house was built, I kept them intact, working within the room's existing architecture and hewing toward tradition.

And believe me, the aesthetic traditions of Lake Forest are worth keeping. This is, after all, where legendary architect David Adler created some of his most important homes. Great taste ran in his family: His sister, interior designer Frances Elkins, also did quite a bit of work here, and was famous for throwing a little extra glamour and a sense of modern verve into her brother's more buttoned-up, classical buildings. I paid homage to her here by using her famous Loop chairs—which she designed in Chicago in 1930— as hostess chairs.

Also casting a spell: the Iksel "Eastern Eden" wallpaper that I selected for its robin's egg blue background. So fresh, and so pretty! The showhouse was originally planned to open in spring, and that color felt really hopeful after a long, dreary winter. To add another unexpected element, I lacquered the ceiling. It's important to treat ceilings in a compelling way. In a pale, pale pink, this one was like sunset in the wide midwestern sky. ✷

RIGHT A custom chandelier from Coleen & Company has just the right amount of glitz, providing a foil for the Iksel chinoiserie wallpaper without being too much of a departure from the original soul of the house. I flanked a traditional mahogany table with antique Louis XVI side chairs that will never go out of style.

OPPOSITE Loop chairs created in Chicago in the 1930s by famed local designer Frances Elkins are so sculptural, they embody the term *eye candy*. To give them a modern contrast, I had them reupholstered in an abstract cubist fabric by Miles Redd for Schumacher that complements the room's color palette while adding a little zing. Lucite brackets create perches for artist Tommy Mitchell's tole flowers without detracting from the chinoiserie.

RIGHT I thought the home's original built-in China cabinet was the most endearing thing (not to mention highly practical in a dining room), so I had to keep it. But I did something unexpected: I had the exterior painted to match the millwork, but the interior is a Prussian blue lacquer. Such a lovely surprise every time it's opened!

SLIM AARONS WOMEN

SLIM AARONS *Style*

PALM BE

PALM BI

AN ENTERTAINING STORY

BEACHSIDE | WINDSOR

BEACHSIDE | WINDSOR

PALM BEACH POLISH

A LUSH, VERDANT SUNROOM

OPPOSITE To give your space a real sense of place in a vacation home, don't forget to include the books on display. Few of us want to read about skiing in St. Moritz when we're in one of the ultimate seafront towns! Here, I curated a selection of Palm Beach-ready tomes—all in Caribbean colors.

FOR A SMALL TOWN—population 8,921—Palm Beach has an outsized reputation. Its name is as instantly recognizable as Paris or New York, Buenos Aires or Tokyo. And just like those legendary cities, it has a singular sense of style. After all, for decades, everyone from presidents to movie stars from the golden age of Hollywood has kicked up their heels in this Florida hamlet. Naturally, when I designed this sunroom at the Kips Bay Decorator Show House Palm Beach, I knew it was imperative to create a sense of place. Like packing your sunscreen and your most glamorous sunglasses when you vacation here, it was a *must*.

Palm Beach has a very specific aesthetic and energy. Across the board, when people conjure this town in their minds, they have visions of pinks and greens, soft yellows and Lilly Pulitzer. To design a sunroom that suited the locale, I didn't want to do anything obvious, but needed to make sure I was honoring the true spirit of this storied town. It wouldn't make sense to have a heavy color palette of brown, red, and navy blue in a town beloved for its sunny weather and happy, tropical disposition. Still, I wanted it to feel like a fresh interpretation of that quintessential Palm Beach style. A tall order!

The first place I turned for inspiration was one of my style icons: Billy Baldwin. The aesthetic visionary touted as "the dean of decorators" and the man behind the slipper chair knew how to combine femininity with a crispness that's forever modern. (Proof he was fabulous: His decorating clients included John F. Kennedy's White House, Cole Porter, Pauline de Rothschild, Diana Vreeland . . . shall I go on?)

Baldwin's work achieved what I hope to achieve in my own projects: a level of timelessness. His interiors were polished and forever elegant. They had a bit of restraint, in that they leaned a little bit more masculine. He didn't use a ton of pattern, but employed color in a really powerful and intentional way. His rooms were also often monochromatic, an approach I used in this sunroom, where my hero color was green. All of the textiles here are either white or green, and we limited ourselves to two patterns—a dogwood leaf and ticking stripe. For the most part, the room reads as leafy, so much so that I call it "Green Gardens"—a play on an iconic home, Grey Gardens. It felt like a nod to Billy and the way he put together such fresh spaces.

Here, to do something interesting as the wall treatment, we sheathed the walls in a natural grasscloth wall covering, then had a custom trellis built on top of it. (Bonus: This helped hide imperfect stucco, in addition to making anyone standing in the room feel deliciously enveloped in it.) Because I wanted it to feel slightly more modern, instead of running the "treillage" or trelliswork in a diamond pattern, I chose to run it in a square pattern, resulting in a much more crisp and graphic effect.

This being Palm Beach, I had to include a bit of vintage—it's practically legally required. I found the pair of rattan chairs and ottomans locally and love how they seem to flirt with the petite custom slipper chairs I had made. What better perches for some iced tea and a few rounds of backgammon? ✳

RIGHT I've long adored lattice for giving a room jaw-dropping depth of field. It also provides a subtle reference to some of history's most stunning rooms, such as Bunny Mellon's garden shed on her 4,000-acre Virginia estate. But it doesn't come cheap. Using it on the ceiling in this sunroom helped create a truly enveloping feeling. The light fixture and lamps here are from my own collection for Visual Comfort and bring a modern element you might not expect in a garden room.

LEFT I originally selected a leafier green color for the upholstery of that sofa, but as luck would have it, the fabric was backordered. Given the time constraints of a showhouse, we had to pivot to this green, which is a couple of shades lighter—and which quickly became a happy accident. Something about it feels a little more "Palm Beach."

OPPOSITE Every vacation home needs a game table where you can put down your phone and get engrossed in mahjong or bridge (just ensure great lighting and comfy seats, in case the game goes into the wee hours). I loved the custom valances we designed with tape trim for the window treatments here: They brought another layer of architecture to the room.

OPPOSITE
I often say that great rooms need something living to really come to life—plants, pets, or children! They instantly provide a sense of life and natural beauty that can do so much for a room and its "dead zones," like an otherwise empty corner. Shown here: bird of paradise, which looks a bit like something Henri Rousseau would have conjured for a painting.

RIGHT I like to make sure even the smallest details reflect their locale. Here, we arranged hand-blown Italian glassware from my shop, Paloma & Co, and a bevy of water options within a woven natural fiber tray.

TAKING CARE
OF BUSINESS

MAKE YOUR WORKPLACE
WORK FOR YOU

OPPOSITE Be sure to make your office speak to your personal aesthetic. We recently upgraded to a larger design studio, but in our former office, you'll see that I married modern with traditional in this meeting spot. Brno chairs and a tulip table look sleek against seagrass rugs and leftover chinoiserie panels I had framed in gilt bamboo (the perfect pairing!).

YOU KNOW THAT CONCEPT of a "bad hair day"—when your coiffure is less than ideal, and then the rest of the day follows suit? That same thing can happen when it comes to the design of your workplace. If your office is beautiful and tidy—in line with your inspirations and motivations—you'll watch your productivity soar.

Our former office was tucked into our retail shop, and it was rapidly becoming too hectic and chaotic . . . and far too cramped for our burgeoning team. We were bursting at the seams! So when we saw that this adjacent cottage in Houston's River Oaks neighborhood became available, we snapped it up immediately. The century-old Craftsman had many former lives, including as a boot maker's shop, a Pilates studio, and a private home. We love that it's surrounded by lush gardens and other creative businesses, also housed in former cottages—including a creative marketing agency and a wonderful Italian restaurant. It creates a buzzing sense of community at all hours.

As designers, we did, of course, do a little nip and tuck to our new cottage office so it would be all the more inspiring to us. We topped the gray painted subfloor with custom wall-to-wall seagrass carpeting so the space would instantly feel more complete. We painted the walls and exposed ceiling beams in my go-to shade of white—Benjamin Moore's White Dove, which works in just about every space and has the right amount of warmth and depth. Because natural light is fairly limited in this studio, we installed museum-quality LED track lights hidden between the beams that mimic daylight.

Now, creating a workable floor plan in seven hundred square feet is no easy task—especially in this case, when it needed to include a common work area for my design team, a conference area for presentations, a resource library, a powder room, and my own private office. But when you stick to a limited color palette and streamlined silhouettes, it can become seamless. We opted for beautiful, hard-wearing furniture and finish choices wherever possible—such as the soft antique gilt mirror hung above the vanity in the powder bath. Or the Brno chairs, which were designed by Mies van der Rohe and Lilly Reich in 1929, around the same time our cottage was built. I found them at auction and scooped them up for a song; they were being sold from a former law office, and I bought twelve for the price of a new pair! It was years ago, and at the time, I didn't have a purpose for them . . . but it was too good a deal to pass up. Keep that in mind as you design your workplace. It's always wise to give yourself room to grow (and keep extra chairs handy), because your business may flourish even faster than you think.

I prefer my personal work spaces to be super crisp and clean (and obviously tasteful and chic!), so I selected a calming neutral color palette and kept it simple. If our office were designed with a riot of pattern and color, it would distract me. It's similar to the type of music you choose to listen to when you work. I love all types of music, but when I'm really trying to get into the zone, I prefer songs that are upbeat without many lyrics. I can't have too much stimulation in my environment if I need to focus on my own imagination.

Ensuring you have the setup to stay organized is vital, because, as any small-business CEO will tell you, paperwork adds up—even in the digital age. We splurged by

RIGHT Good lighting is integral to any successful workspace, as anyone who has ever toiled under a fluorescent overhead glow in an office park can attest. We used various sources of light here: table lamps, a gilded iron and white glass lantern designed by Suzanne Kasler for Visual Comfort, and even LEDs tucked within the open ceiling beams that have a daylight feel.

hiring a professional organizer, a totally worthwhile investment, to help us hone the system in our library. Inside our cabinets, we installed pull-out drawers to house and organize all of our fabric samples. Custom-made acrylic dividers with labels ensure our vendors are properly categorized, and it all tucks away out of sight behind neat-as-a-pin cabinet doors. It's nice not to have to see it all the time, because while it looks perfect on day one, eventually it may get a little messy, even if only momentarily.

We recently moved to an even larger space, but we loved having our office in this building—it was a happy space for us. It was calm and peaceful, and we felt like we could focus here. A testament to that is the fact that even when we had the option of working from home, a lot of my team chose to come in. Like great colleagues, a great workplace is magnetic. ✳

RIGHT Every office needs a library of books that will inspire you to greater career heights. We keep ours out for inspiration, and organize some of the necessary clutter, like fabric samples, behind closed cabinet doors. Painting the walls Benjamin Moore's White Dove made them a warm backdrop for all manner of art.

OPPOSITE Proof that it's all about the mix: In our former office's powder room, we hung an antique mirror over a marble-topped vanity we found at Home Depot. (A prescient move for a growing business: We could take the mirror with us when we moved to a larger office space, but the vanity would have to stay . . . no need to overly invest in it.) I added a pretty faucet and accessories and called it a day.

PALOMA & CO

SHOP IN STYLE

OPPOSITE My Houston shop, Paloma & Co, is always a treasure trove of timeless finds that are curated and displayed like a de facto museum (one you can take home with you!). Many of my favorite things are here, including framed intaglios inspired by ancient Rome and textured terra-cotta vases.

I'VE WANTED TO HAVE MY OWN STORE ever since I was a little girl, playing make-believe shopkeeper with my toy cash register. Now that I'm a designer, I love nothing more than finding incredible things on my travels across the globe and curating them for our clients and customers. After amassing enough treasures on my travels to fill a couple of storage units, I decided to open a curated brick-and-mortar store, Paloma & Co, in 2019. We soon realized that about 50 percent of our business was coming from Instagram, so we launched an e-commerce website about six months after opening our doors. It was just in the nick of time! When COVID-19 hit in March 2020, clients tucked safely away at home were longing to redecorate. It was a catalyst for a huge amount of growth.

Our mission at Paloma & Co—which recently moved to a new, larger location—is to curate captivating, unexpected things for the home. That ranges from the substantial (say, a French antique Louis Philippe commode made of burled walnut) to hostess gifts (like candles from Australia's SoH Melbourne, fragranced with whiffs of the natural world, from jasmine and fig to vetiver). I love that the store affords us the opportunity to help a broader range of people by having a variety of offerings, whether it's full-scale, full-service interior design or stocking a curated assortment of finishing touches that customers can quickly stroll in to get.

The best retail experiences are brimming with design lessons. Just as we did in our adjacent office, we wanted our shop to feel super crisp, clean, and welcoming. Almost like museum curators, we didn't want the environment to detract or distract from the pieces in the shop, so we have a pale white oak floor and simple Parsons-style shelving. Throughout, antique treasures mingle with the sleek and new, with a dose of live topiaries and flower arrangements for good measure.

We painted all the walls in our go-to Benjamin Moore White Dove, because one of my biggest passions has become our biggest sales category: original artwork by emerging artists. We represent artists from every corner of the United States. Our walls and shelves often include abstract paintings by William McLure and expressionist landscapes by Kristin Blakeney (both from Birmingham, Alabama); Nashville paper and silk artist Kayce Hughes; and graffiti-inspired painter Ron Giusti of Portland, Oregon.

And whether I'm shopping at the Marché aux Puces in Paris or working with dealers in Europe, I try really hard to find unexpected things you won't see anywhere else. From the aquamarine tumblers handblown in Italy that I discovered at my favorite Italian restaurant in Paris, to the matchbox made from Congan zebrawood, I want everything to feel like a "find." That's honestly one of my very favorite parts of my job: the thrill of the hunt and then, if you're very lucky, the score—unearthing something amazing you weren't expecting to see. Is there anything better? ✳

RIGHT You can tell I love combining historical touches and modern art every time you step foot in Paloma & Co (which has recently moved to a new, larger location than the boutique shown here) or shop our website. Chinoiserie garden stools mingle with abstracts by Kayce Hughes; textural rush baskets with marbleized Paul Schneider trays.

FOLLOWING Using a crisp and clean color palette on your shelves—such as one that's limited to blacks, whites, and golds, or botanical greens, shown here—is an easy way to ensure it is eye-catching. Vary textures and eras for interest, and always aim to include the unexpected . . . like our scalloped bowl cut from solid marble or polka-dotted hand-blown glass party tumblers.

PARIS CHIC

INVITING INTERIORS

Lee Radziwill
ASSOULINE

AD *at* 100

AD *at* 100

SHORE THING

AN ART-FILLED
RETREAT BY THE SEA

OPPOSITE The colors of the living space are muted and soft, without too much jarring pattern—including a low-pile Elizabeth Eakins rug that's very easy to live with. That allowed us to use texture and the client's curated collection of unexpected contemporary art to tell an interesting story not often seen in an ocean house (case in point: Ellsworth Kelly's *The Seine* at left).

THERE IS SOMETHING ETERNALLY BEWITCHING about the ocean: the salty air, the skies that stretch on endlessly to the horizon. It should perhaps come as no surprise, then, that in the height of the pandemic my Texas-based client had a yen for the sandy coastline of his home state of New Jersey. In fact, he missed it so much that he impulse-bought a little something for his wife and their two darling girls: a beach house on the Jersey Shore they could use as their dreamy escape.

He was very passionate about the process and had a clear idea of what he wanted to see in this house, which was really fun and different. His goal was for the interiors to feel relaxed and coastal with an East Coast accent. Ultimately, we wanted the design to lean toward a New England look: tailored and polished and elegant, but in a casual way. I think we were able to achieve that. The home is timeless but has some unexpected touches that tell the story of the family and make it truly interesting.

Because beach houses can easily become clichéd—with a shell lamp here, a nautical rope mirror there—we worked hard to give the home a coastal aesthetic while avoiding the obvious route and any semblance of cheesiness. We took a lot of our cues from the nature beyond the windows, especially the color palette: the cerulean blues and fresh greens of sky and sea. The colors are more muted in the formal spaces, such as the living room and primary bedroom. But they become more saturated and modern in the hangout spots, like the family room.

We clad the latter in warm French white oak panel-ing, which makes it feel a little like the hold of a yacht. (Actually, not a single wall in this home is plain Sheetrock! Every single wall surface is either shiplap or wallpaper, from the Japanese waves in a powder room to the leafy canopy in the laundry room.) The desire was for the family room to feel super cozy and inviting, the kind of place where you want to curl up and watch a movie together. While we carried the aforementioned oak paneling into this room, we ran it horizontally rather than vertically to set it apart from the rest of the house and add architecture. A streamlined Italian sofa and sleek modern light choices, including articulating sconces that turn myriad ways, help set the mood—no overhead lights allowed.

This client is a contemporary art fanatic and has amassed a collection worthy of the MoMA. Hung in the family room: Ed Ruscha's *Cold Beer Beautiful Girls*—a nod to the women in his life. The client sweetly said, "People might think that's a crazy art choice, but it's basically my life. I'm passionate about my beer and my wine, and my beautiful wife and daughters." Presiding over the great room, a quartet of works by Anish Kapoor and an Ells-worth Kelly piece give the space an edge. In the foyer, we juxtaposed an Elliott Puckette etched gesso-and-ink board with relics from a shipwreck. Not exactly your standard-is-sue beach house "art," which is just the way we like it.

One of my favorite rooms in this home is the kitchen, which has lofty twenty-foot-high ceilings. For the back-splash and countertop, we selected a Calacatta Borghini marble for its white and creamy gold veining, which mimics the movement and froth of the ocean waves. In a room that's so crisp and clean otherwise, it was a nice op-portunity to add interest. I like to have countertop edges mitered to make stone slabs feel crisp and more substan-tial. We paired the beautiful stone with a polished nickel faucet (that metal choice is much more forgiving when it comes to water splashes than gleaming chrome). Rush rope and leather stools and masculine pendants worthy of a barnacled boat add to the seaworthy feel.

Because the home sits just a few houses in from the water, we were careful to select outdoor furniture for the terraces that could stand up to the salt air and seafront squalls. We had a lot of custom furniture made from teak and powder-coated metal—each piece with a bespoke cover that could keep it safely under wraps through New Jersey's inevitably frigid winter season. Of course, some degree of patina will come over time, and it should. It's like the brass of a ship's wheel that's been burnished by sea captains over the years and made all the more beauti-ful because of it. ✳

OPPOSITE Sleek light fixtures and graphic modern art add so much personality to the living space; it turns it on its head a bit. This series of four is by Anish Kapoor, and I love how it juxtaposes against furniture with a tailored New England coastal feel, such as the American mission-style coffee table.

FOLLOWING The architectural bones of the home are very classic, so I used interesting accent pieces—such as graphic side tables and a low-slung Kerry Joyce accent chair—to bring in some doses of unpredictable character. That's key to keeping things interesting.

THE NEW CLASSIC HOME

ABOVE & OPPOSITE The traditional cabinetry we specified for the kitchen gave us the opportunity to do something more interesting on the counters and backsplash with movement and color, such as the Calacatta Borghini shown here. I like a thicker countertop, so will normally have the edges mitered to give the illusion of a chunkier 2-centimeter slab. We selected the pendant lights above the island because they felt like marine fixtures, or something you would find on a boat. And their scale worked really nicely with the expansive 20-foot height of the ceiling! Opting for leather seats on the cerused white oak and rush rope stools made them both comfortable and very easy to live with.

LEFT In the powder room, Gracie's Silvered Waves wallpaper reminds me of a famous circa-1831 wood-block print by Katsushika Hokusai, *The Great Wave off Kanagawa*. It's our nod to a beach house— but in a more ele- vated way—and it envelops you in the space.

OPPOSITE There was no architect working with us on this spec home; our team updated and customized it where we could to make it feel as if it had been here for decades. In the powder room, I added character by using mixed metals and exposed pipes under the vanity— little design details not often found in new builds.

ABOVE The primary bedroom suite is on the third floor, and it's the only room up there. Like any centuries-old garret room, it has lots of odd ceiling angles that feel very choppy, with an ultra-low pitch in certain places . . . a major design challenge! My fix was to tent the room in a striped wall covering so it would feel cozy and inviting, and translate all the space's angles into something more pleasing to the eye.

OPPOSITE A faux bois ceramic lamp by Christopher Spitzmiller looks a bit like driftwood. I loved the idea of bringing in texture in a room with so much pattern—the matte white feels like a good, clean contrast.

LEFT We were originally going to use this hand-blocked seafoam and ochre linen fabric from Claremont on the bed's custom European pillows, but the client loved it so much he asked if we could utilize it in a bigger way. We employed it on the drapery as well at his behest. I adored working with him: I never wanted to push him too far in an ultra-feminine direction, and then he would end up pushing me!

OPPOSITE Every bedroom requires a plush, comfortable chair for reading and chatting about the day. Limit any objet on the cocktail table next to it to two pieces max; you'll need space for a book (and a cappuccino or gin and tonic).

OPPOSITE The primary suite's bathroom is super-classic with traditional materials at every turn, such as chunky marble cladding the floors and shower. We selected reeded glass Art Deco–inspired sconces for over the vanity. They emit a soft, forgiving light.

RIGHT Because the freestanding soaking tub is such a conventional shape, I set a sculptural occasional chair alongside it. The cerused oak finish adds a bit of warmth to the space, and it's the perfect spot for setting extra towels.

OPPOSITE Their two girls share a room when the family is in New Jersey, so we made it extra sweet with a palette of pinks, blues, and lavender. He told me the girls love their room and spend lots of time playing with their puppies on the rug in there! The drapery textile is by southern textile company Virginia Kraft, named for the artist's maternal grandmother; it feels so feminine and fresh.

ABOVE My client chose these pieces of art specifically for his daughters. They depict Wildwood, New Jersey, where five miles of wide, sandy shores have drawn generations of families living large every summer. For an East Coast beach house, I felt bobbin spindle beds would be the perfect choice.

SHORE THING

163

OPPOSITE
I selected a mirror that echoes the wavy lines of a scallop shell for the girls' en-suite bathroom. Monogrammed towels are a fun touch in a kids' private bathroom; it helps them feel like it's very much a room of their own.

RIGHT In little girls' bedrooms, I can't get enough of small-print floral linens and scalloped details. Childhood is so precious and fleeting—I always try to make their bedrooms as dreamy and delight-ful as possible!

OPPOSITE Who doesn't love a bunk room? In this seven-bedroom home, two bedrooms are bunk rooms . . . ideal for hosting out-of-town family and friends aplenty. I found this wallpaper and fabric by Mally Skok, which has little hints of fuchsia throughout and is the hero of the room. You think it's navy and cream at first glance, and then the pink surprises you upon closer inspection.

RIGHT The florals we selected seemed to demand a really crisp, clean graphic accent, so we chose cloud-white bedding trimmed in black. The built-in sconces, shiplap siding, and ladder in this bunk room give it the feel of an old ship.

ABOVE & OPPOSITE Bedrooms don't need an ocean view to get the relaxed feel of a Vacationland. Hanging a choice piece of art— like this one, where bathers dip in clear turquoise water—can have a similarly calming effect. I find shiplap an especially fitting wall treatment by the ocean, because historically, its overlapping wood joints were used to create a waterproof seal on seaworthy ships.

FOLLOWING This inner hallway's stocky, round ceiling lights feel a bit like porthole windows. I've always loved the scale of this iconic fig leaf wallpaper by Peter Dunham, so I put it to good use in the laundry room, where it brings the outdoors in and helps the otherwise utilitarian space feel fresh. The light fixture supplies an old New England schoolhouse vibe.

RIGHT This is technically the family room, but we always called it Rhett's room—that's our client. It's tailor-made for him to curl up with a cold beer and beautiful girls, as the Ed Ruscha art piece says (and which he chose in homage to his wife and daughters), for movie nights. French white oak walls are laid horizontally here to envelop the room. With the handmade textiles and the clean-lined Italian sofa, it's all very masculine and modern.

OPPOSITE An Elliott Puckette painting and chest made in nineteenth-century Sweden stand watchword over the foyer. The alabaster lamp, stack of books, and fresh-cut blooms help soften the look.

RIGHT A trio of plates found in a shipwreck-turned-tabletop sculptures are appropriate for a beach house, but so unexpected. They're wonderfully textural and, perched on black metal stands, very much worthy of an exhibition at the Metropolitan Museum of Art.

SUSANNA SALK

AT HOME IN THE ENGLISH COUNTRYSIDE
DESIGNERS AND THEIR DOGS

PENNOYER · WALKER
ROWDY MEADOW

HOUSE
LAND
ART

LEFT You can see the ocean from this outdoor dining room—and smell the salty air. We treated it like an indoor space, cozying it up with a rug underfoot and a plush banquette with plenty of throw pillows for comfort. A trio of tabletop lanterns ensure a warm glow into the evening.

OPPOSITE It's possible to nod to the always-inspiring sea on your tabletop in a subtle way. Here, the place setting includes a handwoven rattan napkin ring, an easy-to-hold seagrass-wrapped cup, and a marine blue drinking glass, all from my shop, Paloma & Co.

ORGANIC MODERN

REIMAGINING THE
FARMHOUSE TRADITION

OPPOSITE The homeowners of this country house have a very pared-down aesthetic: they favor a monochromatic palette, clean lines, and a mix of old and new. That's evidenced in every oversized room and even the smallest details, such as the built-in shelves at left.

NEWLY BUILT HOMES sometimes get a bad rap, but they shouldn't. If done well, they're like a painstakingly designed couture gown versus a hand-me-down that might be in desperate need of tailoring. Given the option, who wouldn't choose the former? When my longtime clients announced that they were done with city life and longed to build a farmhouse from the ground up on expansive acreage in Fulshear, Texas, we were all too delighted to help.

We got involved with the architecture from the beginning, meeting with the residential architect biweekly to review progress and weigh in on details large and small. We had a lot of input on the cabinetry and millwork, as well as issues of space distribution and flow. For some reason, this architect didn't have any interest in hallway corridors, so I had to put my proverbial foot down. This home demanded the classical approach of a hall. Not only did the client have a deep art collection begging for wall space, but the house also needed that age-old element of coziness.

Our biggest challenge, though, had to do with the fact that this was out in the country. Being far from an urban center is great when you want to feel like you're living in an Old Master's oil landscape painting—here, the abundant parcel was practically a nature preserve, dotted with hundred-year-old oak and pecan trees. But rural living can be somewhat tricky when it comes to the art of home-building itself. The builders we worked with were wonderful, but not necessarily accustomed to doing this style of architecture. There was a bit of trial and error to get things like the slurry application on the stone exterior just right. Thankfully, practice made perfect!

When it came to the interiors, our client asked us for a simple, pared-down aesthetic. We didn't want it to read as that farmhouse vernacular that is—let's be honest—a little overplayed. So instead, we designed an elevated version that I call "modern organic." It is still contemporary and clean-lined, but there's a lot of warmth that comes as a result of using natural and local materials, including reclaimed Texas white oak, marble, and French limestone worthy of Château de Chambord.

It helped that we built so many elements from scratch, combining the best of Old World and new. Even in the powder room, you'll see modern elements come to light in centuries-old ways. The walls are Venetian plaster, which is made with fired limestone and has added depth and texture to interiors since the days of the Roman Empire. We designed the floating vanity out of Nero Marquina marble to look super graphic, then juxtaposed it with a simple vessel sink and an unlacquered brass wall-mounted faucet. After dusk, those Murano-inspired sconces splay intricate patterns of light on the wall. Exquisite!

Because the kitchen is one of the first things you see in the largely open floor plan, we injected functional requirements with as much beauty as possible. Texas white oak flooring and reclaimed beams on the ceiling add a lot of warmth to the space, especially paired with the marble that we ran all the way up the wall behind the plaster hood. To ensure that the room feels layered, sleek cabinets and Kelly Wearstler pendants bring a touch of modernity. We also installed a waterfall-edge island in a crisp white quartz that's nearly impossible to mar. (Some clients love the look of marble and don't mind when it patinas and etches over time, but not this client! I always say—"Know

RIGHT My client has always loved the work of William McLure from Birmingham, Alabama, and followed him on Instagram for ages. So we commissioned this piece for the dining room of her last house, and it happened to suit this wall perfectly . . . a testament to being true to yourself and your tastes, wherever you roam.

thyself!") Not a problem: Using marble on the perimeter counters and quartz on the workhorse of an island gave us the best of both worlds.

In the main living room, the seating is all meant for lounging: extra-deep for comfort, and swaddled in a nubby bouclé. The iron doors (made locally by Atelier Domingue) provide a beautiful vista out to the garden and pool, not to mention they allow light to flow in free-range. The tall fireplace is made of the same Nero Marquina marble we employed in the powder room—just one of many decor bread crumbs that weave throughout the house, tying each room to the next. Above the monochromatic palette of whites and creams and grays, we needed a bit of an edge. Given the volume of the room—those are seventeen-foot ceilings!—and the tall white walls and airy millwork, contrast was key, so I chose a graphic chandelier with inky black shades. By bouncing light off the ceiling, the fixture creates a wonderful glow that's as inviting as it gets.

One of my favorite elements of this room is the painting above the sideboard; it's a lesson in staying true to yourself. We commissioned this piece—by Birmingham, Alabama, artist William McLure, whom my client had followed on Instagram for ages—for the dining room of her last house, and it happened to work perfectly here. Keeping her treasured artwork helped make her current home feel like a personal evolution, rather than a completely jarring contrast from a previous life. It's a testament to investing in things you truly love, because they'll likely stay with you for the long haul! Shakespeare had it right: To thine own design tastes be true. ✳

LEFT This is the more formal of the clients' two living rooms, but it's still very casual, with the TV front and center and deep, comfy seating (like nubby bouclé armchairs) ready for lounging. One of my favorite elements of this space are the iron windows and doors created by local Houston company Atelier Domingue; their black muntins put a stunning focus on the pool and spacious acreage beyond the glass.

OPPOSITE The entrance hall sets the tone for the entire house, with a striking abstract by Joelle Somero from Michigan, stone walls and a striking, clean-lined lantern.

RIGHT This nook below the iron stair rail could easily have felt empty and a little cold, if not for this abstract art piece by Brian Coleman and the textural earthenware pot bursting with fresh-cut, verdant branches.

LEFT The dining room is situated toward the back of the house, with oversized windows on three sides overlooking panoramic views of the grounds with hundred-year-old oak trees and pecan trees as far as the eye can see. We installed a glimmering crystal chandelier inspired by a French antique to play up the ceiling height without blocking the views, while the chunky wood table juxtaposes against tailored and feminine Louis XVI side chairs.

LEFT The kitchen gets a ton of use, so it needed to be truly functional yet gorgeous as well. In keeping with the fact that the client wanted to use as many natural materials and finishes as possible, the flooring is Texas white oak, and reclaimed barn beams stud the ceiling. While the perimeter counters are marble, we decided to utilize quartz on the waterfall-edge island because it's practically indestructible and less likely to stain.

FOLLOWING Hidden away behind their spotless primary kitchen, the homeowners have a second "catering" kitchen where they do much of their actual cooking. In the mudroom, we decided on flat-front cabinets paired with a beautiful French limestone floor, which adds warmth to the space. The stainless-steel sink is a workhorse; she can do all kinds of things there, from cutting flowers to washing their two French bulldogs.

ORGANIC MODERN

189

LEFT Most of the house is light and bright, so in this office we veered into a moodier scheme. The walls are painted Farrow & Ball's Hague Blue, a color both the client and I love for its depth and neutral gray undertone. It's stunning, but not too bold.

OPPOSITE The perpendicular lines of this built-in oak bookcase and cabinet are a serene backdrop for curated art and sculptural accessories. We limited the color palette of the books here to white, gray, and black for a tranquil feel.

LEFT This family loves to entertain; they're the people in their friend group who are always hosting game parties and celebrating birthdays. That's one reason we created a showstopper of a bar. It's a masculine counterpoint to the kitchen, and echoes a few other spots in the home with its Nero Marquina marble.

OPPOSITE To emphasize the natural beauty of Nero Marquina marble—which looks a bit like lightning zigzagging across the night sky—we had beautiful floating shelves made of it: the perfect perch for displaying stemware and glasses in an artful way. The room's brass accents and patterns in the wool rug serve to cozy up the space wonderfully.

OPPOSITE
The walls of this powder room are done in Venetian plaster to supply warmth and texture. We custom-designed the floating vanity out of Nero Marquina marble, which feels so graphic and cool, and paired it with a simple vessel sink and unlacquered brass wall-mounted faucet and antiqued mirror with Murano glass–inspired sconces.

RIGHT These nine abstract pieces on Japanese paper are by the same artist I've displayed in my dining room at home in Houston: Jane Timberlake Cooper. They have a lot of texture and movement, but there's a softness about them. In a grid, though, they become graphic and strong: the ideal comple-ment to this hallway between the kitchen and family room.

RIGHT If the kids have friends over, they often beeline for this second living or family room. The ceilings aren't quite as high as they are in the main living space, but it's still as expansive as Texas itself (to give you an idea, that custom chandelier is an enormous five feet across).

FOLLOWING The primary bathroom has similar elements to the rest of the home—blond oak wood, limestone, and even marble slabs surrounding the mirror—but it's a little more glamorous, thanks to the light fixture and modern finishes. The primary suite is awash in her beloved monochromatic color palette: blacks, whites, and creams. We delighted in the details, such as the graphically patterned lumbar pillow on the velvet bed and trim on the leading edge of the drapery.

LEFT The architect used a lot of Texas limestone on the exterior facade, which practically glows after nightfall and creates such a warm, welcoming approach.

MOUNTAIN MAGIC

EMBRACING
THE ALPINE AIR

OPPOSITE In a smaller home like this 2,000-square-foot Cashiers, North Carolina, vacation house, sky-high windows work wonders to allow much-needed light to flow. We emphasized the peaceful setting with leafy and neutral hues and earthy finishes (and by painting the existing brown wood paneling Benjamin Moore's Decorator's White).

OF ALL THE MOUNTAIN TOWNS in all the world, Cashiers ranks high, at least in my estimation. It straddles the misty waterfalls and lush forests of North Carolina's Gorges State Park and Panthertown Valley Backcountry Area (otherwise known as the Yosemite of the East, thanks to its Ansel Adams–worthy granite domes). It's also home to the High Hampton Inn Historic District, with a 1922 lakeside inn and Tom Fazio–designed golf course. No wonder it's been a favorite getaway of Atlantans for generations, especially as an escape from Georgia's sweltering summer heat.

While my clients' new Cashiers cabin had all the charms required of a Blue Ridge Mountain retreat, including verdant woodlands out the windows and an imposing stone fireplace that soared up to the rafters, it wasn't exactly camera-ready when they bought it. Built in the 1990s, the four-bedroom house had beige wall-to-wall carpet; dark wood paneling; dated, builder-grade kitchen and baths; and an overall feeling of gloomy darkness. It was nothing to write home about. And believe me, when you're on vacation with your family, you want to have wonderful reasons to write home!

These Atlanta-based clients have teenage kids, so creating a space they could share unforgettable memories in was a must. They gave me a very clear directive that they wanted it to feel casual and comfortable, because they knew they would come here to entertain friends and family (often with their kids' friends in tow). Functionality was paramount. We wanted it to feel really crisp and clean—a more modern version of a little mountain cabin. The first order of business was painting every inch of the place. (I learned an important design lesson early on: There are few ills that a coat of white paint can't fix!) Here, we used Benjamin Moore's Decorator's White on practically every wall. People find selecting the right white very difficult, but this particular hue is one of my go-to colors because of its cool, flattering undertones.

When you look beyond the windows in the great room, you see forest scenery in every direction. Such a gorgeous muse! Those woods became the home's focal point, kicking off a palette of neutrals with green accents that would bring the outdoors in. Throughout, we tried to weave a cohesive thread between what was happening just outside the doors and the interior, using as many local, organic options as possible. We put as much seating as we could into this living room, working with natural materials that felt appropriate for the locale and its earthy scenery—linens, reclaimed wood, and iron. It's all fitting for the North Carolina mountains but features more clean lines than the usual. Along those lines, using a smattering of black was key. It grounds the room, adds a graphic touch, and generally serves to balance whatever else is going on. In this case, everything is so crisp and light and airy that you need something dark with visual heft to bring it together. Without black, this room would sort of fall off the page. The vibe would be completely different.

Above it all, we hung a double-ring iron chandelier, which brought the modern mountain aesthetic we were going for. Because it's essentially a two-story room, we needed something with a large scale and diameter to suit the space. Another of my favorite decor moments came courtesy of the local fire chief, who dropped off the stacked wood that adds such a cozy—and useful—touch

RIGHT Casual, mountain-appropriate materials reflect the locale, including the reclaimed wood coffee table, linens, and a tiered iron chandelier that draws your eyes up to the rafters and had the simplicity of the clean, alpine aesthetic we were aiming for. My client found the Lalanne-inspired sheep and it was so endearing, we had to keep it.

to the stone fireplace wall. Framing the picture windows are botanical prints of flora that look like something you could pluck from the ground in the forest outside. Underfoot, we placed a sisal rug, which is a little softer than seagrass and available in more hues. I personally love a natural-fiber rug and use them frequently. They're just the right amount of casual, and more livable than a riot of colorful patterns, typically. (Bonus: They can be Fiber Sealed, so they'll clean up just as well as wool.)

Just as the brightness of noon makes the inky midnight sky all the more transfixing, we had to find something to balance the home's white walls. In the galley kitchen and wet bar, we went dark, painting the simple cabinetry with Sherwin-Williams's moody Iron Ore. Not only does the color serve to stabilize the airier spaces, but it sets the stage for the greenery beyond the windows to truly pop— just as Mother Nature intended. ✳

OPPOSITE Just about every room I design needs a hint of black to lend gravitas and balance whatever else is going on, and that's just as true at the dining table as anywhere else.

LEFT Our clients found the sweet horse and sheep art piece in the dining room, a nod to their neighborhood of Sheep Laurel. It provides a focal point and cheerful view all year round.

LEFT Just around the corner from the kitchen under the floating staircase, we decided to build a little wet bar. It's very cohesive in tone with the primary cook space (the cabinets are the same hue, Sherwin Williams's Iron Ore) because they're somewhat connected, but so easy to grab a drink from when you're entertaining guests.

OPPOSITE A humble bowl of emerald moss on the coffee table helps bring the outdoors into the living room and feels forever fresh. A pop of green like that is always so welcomed, especially in a neutral environment with a beautiful vista out the windows.

LEFT I use natural-fiber rugs over ornate ones very frequently, because I don't love a riot of pattern. This home is so casual, sisal was a fitting choice.

LEFT We carried the home's restful color palette into the primary bedroom—including chartreuse draperies that felt like a very modern version of green—and used plenty of varied textures. When you have simple architecture and a neutral scheme, you really have to rely on texture to keep things interesting!

OPPOSITE Comfort is of the utmost importance in a sitting area, so I always include a plush down bolster pillow as well as a throw blanket nearby; tuck the latter in a basket to have it on hand without clutter.

LEFT Mixing metals (like we did with the vanity hardware and faucet here) often helps create the feeling that a room was pulled together over the years—a comfortable and welcoming effect. The miniature oil painting also helped warm up the space.

OPPOSITE I often employ an antiqued mirror in a space to provide the heady aura of history. The rope-wrapped unlacquered brass lamp has a similar result in a thoroughly modern shape.

ABOVE One challenge of this home is that the second-story bedrooms, like this girls' room, have severely sloped ceilings. So we kept all our furniture choices on the lower side (such as these sweet spindle beds) and used a Lisa Fine floral fabric as our muse for the unobtrusive color palette.

OPPOSITE This piece by textile designer Paule Marrot—born in Bordeaux, France, in 1902—felt perfect for the room, because I could picture a young lady venturing into the nearby woods and happening upon a little patch of wildflowers just like this one.

OPPOSITE The faux bois wallpaper in the boys' bathroom gives them a bit of a summer camp aesthetic and carries the design thread over from the adjacent bedroom.

ABOVE This boys' room is one of my favorite spaces in the entire house, with its deep, dreamy walls that seem to capture the night sky, Glacier National Park wool Pendleton blankets, and army pillows. A striped dhurrie rug brought in more clean lines to balance the spindled beds. .

IN LIVING COLOR

BRIGHT DAYS AHEAD

OPPOSITE My fun-loving clients' Houston house functions as a buzzing hive for all their family and friends, who frequently come over for big, joyful dinner parties. When the living room is awash in sandy neutrals and serene silhouettes (like this Eero Saarinen Womb Chair), you can go wild with color and pattern in the adjacent play space, as we did here.

SOME PEOPLE ARE AFRAID TO LIVE with vibrant color, perhaps worried that it will be like having a cacophonous roommate who never leaves the house. But I've found that color can be more akin to the best friend you rely on to get through a stressful workday. Employed correctly, it is likely to provide you with a jolt of renewed energy or serene calm when and where you need it most— from happy, welcoming foyers to restful primary bedrooms.

This particular home is unequivocally the most modern project in this book—contemporary to the core. It's also a testament to the power of color to put pep in your step. There is not one corner of the house that wasn't transformed by a mere touch (or a broad, enveloping swath) of jewel-tone hues, including deep rouge pinks and sapphire blues. These long-term clients, a young family with two little girls, could not have been more fun to work with, and their new home, which they built from the ground up, reflects that. They have a very modern, creative sense of style, so it's fitting that they live in Montrose, a neighborhood that's basically Houston's answer to West Hollywood—very hip, with buzzing restaurants, art, and culture at every turn.

We had an unlikely muse for their home's interiors: Copenhagen, a city where my clients rented an apartment and spent an entire dreamy summer. Many of our selections in their home were spurred by their time in Denmark, including the blond oak floors in a herringbone pattern and custom steel doors that separate the living room and playroom. My clients became obsessed with those design details living overseas, so they formed the ultimate take-home souvenir.

The most fun room in this home is arguably the play-room, which we separated from the main living room with the aforementioned steel doors. The clients' extended family lives in the neighborhood, and they host big dinners several nights a week, so the glass playroom doors keep the children's activity within sight of where adults are spending time (and provide a bit of a sound buffer). They had a Missoni Mah Jong sofa in their Copenhagen apartment and were determined to have one here, because they'd fallen in love with its modular style and low, long silhouette (perfect for their girls to jump on). Its saturated, Crayola-bright patterns kicked off the room's entire more-is-more aesthetic. I felt like we might as well go big or go home in this space! The bird-and-butterfly wallpaper felt graphic and modern, but it was nice to bring in a natural element. We echoed it with the butterfly chandelier, which is as delicate and eye-catching as a kaleidoscope of monarchs. The cherry on the sundae, though, is the ribbon piece by Atlanta-based artist Angela Chrusciaki Blehm. It's the perfect contrast to all the feminine details, and instantly draws the eye.

Because the playroom's use of color and pattern was so robust, we used hues in a more minimal way in the adjacent living room. I wanted to make sure that the spaces felt distinct from each other but still played well together . . . they're in full view of each other, after all! The living room's color palette is rooted in neutrals, with jewel-tone accents used in mindful ways, such as in the throw pillows or the banding on the draperies.

One of the most thoroughly "Scandi"-feeling spaces in this home is the entrance hall, where my client's punchy

RIGHT The colors in the playroom are incredibly saturated, and it trickles down from there (you'll see similar hues on the pillows and drapery banding in the adjacent living room). A pixelated-looking light fixture takes the stage here, where calmer colors and clean-lined furniture retreat a bit. It's worth investing in well-made wool rugs, such as this one with circles woven into it at different levels. They're not inexpensive, but they tend to be so durable that they can last for generations.

OPPOSITE A hard-wearing coffee table is all but required in a family home. This one has a slate top and an oak base, and—alongside the black standing lamps and iron French doors—helps ground this airy space. I love that it helped usher more natural materials into this contemporary environment.

RIGHT With the clients' abstract art pieces in Crayola-bright colors in the dining room, we opted for comparatively neutral furniture. The table is extra-long for hosting as many friends and family as possible, and is frequently filled with laughter.

arched art pieces and a cool, architecturally curved mirror are paired with a comparatively humble utilitarian bench. We also juxtaposed color with clean-lined minimalism in the powder room, where the Schumacher Chiang Mai Dragon wall covering pays homage to my clients' Chinese heritage. It's an iconic chinoiserie motif with so much vibrancy that it practically begs to be paired with something sleek, such as this pedestal sink, riveted mirror, and articulating sconces. As always, the beauty is in the details!

As you might expect, no ordinary kitchen would satisfy the cravings of this art-loving family. So, when it came to the cookspace, we opted for unexpected choices that still feel timeless, including warm, flat-paneled walnut cabinetry and a ten-foot-long island with a gleaming waterfall edge and walnut paneling underneath. Over the double basin galley sink, we installed twin faucets. The pairing allows "too many cooks in the kitchen" to proceed happily with their tasks at hand, from prepping serving platters to washing herbs freshly plucked from the garden . . . European living at its best, right here in the heart of Texas. ✳

OPPOSITE There is no powder room that can't be made more charming with wallpaper, and this one—Schumacher's intricate Chiang Mai Dragon—packs a visual wallop. It's busy, traditional, and fresh feeling . . . a rare find.

LEFT You get an instant visual whiff of my clients' summer in Copenhagen when you enter their foyer, with its herringbone blond-wood floors, simple Nordic bench, and a trio of contemporary art pieces they'd collected (the third arch, in blue, is not pictured).

OPPOSITE The warm walnut cabinetry in the kitchen demanded a little dressing up. We installed Zellige Moroccan tile on the wall to add sheen and formality, then went for gleaming polished counters. I didn't mind mixing wood types in this room; like mixed metals, it can give a space dimension and warmth.

RIGHT If you've ever fought to use a faucet, you know how sanity-saving two separate ones set over a lengthy galley sink can be. It allows two people more of a free-range feeling in the kitchen, so one can do prep work while the other tackles the dishes or another task. The acrylic cube art piece in the background is by artist Katherine Houston.

LEFT The primary bedroom is painted in Farrow & Ball's Hague Blue, which we used to give these parents a cozy respite that feels like a departure within a house with mostly white walls. It wasn't hard to land on that color: She loves a jewel tone! And it suited the Lee Jofa fabric I'd found for the lumbar pillow and draperies.

OPPOSITE Their en-suite bath has very similar walnut cabinets to the kitchen, but we brought in unlacquered brass hardware to warm it up a bit. I wanted it to feel slightly mid-century, so installed wall-mounted faucets and Calacatta Viola marble with purple veining.

RESOURCES

ANTIQUES

1st Dibs *1stdibs.com*

Chairish *chairish.com*

Elizabeth Pash Antiques *elizabethpash.com*

Gerald Bland *geraldblandinc.com*

Liz O'Brien *lizobrien.com*

Lucca Antiques *luccaantiques.com*

Old Plank Antiques *oldplank.com*

Paul Bert Serpette Paris *paulbert-serpette.com*

ART

Alexis Walter *alexiswalter.com*

Angela Chrusciaki Blehm *angelachrusciakiblehm.com*

Betsy Senior Fine Art *betsyseniorfineart.com*

Blair Voltz Clarke *voltzclarke.com*

Cristea Roberts Gallery *cristearoberts.com*

Dale Goffigan *dalegoffigan.com*

F.L. Braswell Fine Art *flbfineart.com*

Galerie Maximillian *galeriemax.com*

Hope Lloyd Brown *hopelloydbrown.com*

Jane Timberlake Cooper *janetimberlakecooper.com*

Kasmin Gallery *kasmingallery.com*

Kayce Hughes *kaycehughes.com*

Laura Rathe Fine Art *laurarathe.com*

Leslie Sacks Gallery *lesliesacks.com*

Lindsey J. Porter *lindseyjporter.com*

Miles McEnery Gallery *milesmcenery.com*

Natural Curiosities *naturalcuriosities.com*

Staley-Wise Gallery *staleywise.com*

William McLure *williammclure.com*

Zane Bennett Gallery *zanebennettgallery.com*

DRAPERY & CUSTOM UPHOLSTERY

Chicago Upholstery & Drapery Co. *chicagoupholsterycompany.com*

Dicembrino Upholstery *dicembrinoupholstery.com*

G&S Custom Draperies *gandscustomdraperies.com*

Heine's Custom Draperies *heinescustomdraperies.com*

Neal & Co. Upholstery

The Joseph Company *josephcompany.com*

The Work Room *theworkroomnyc.com*

FABRICS

ALT for Living *altforliving.com*

Brunschwig & Fils *brunschwigfils.com*

Caroline Irving Textiles *carolineirvingtextiles.com*

Casa Branca *casabranca.com*

China Seas *quadrillefabrics.com/chinaseas*

Claremont *claremontfurnishing.com*

Clarence House *clarencehouse.com*

Cowtan & Tout *cowtan.com*

Elizabeth Eakins *elizabetheakins.com*

Holland & Sherry *hollandandsherry.com*

Holly Hunt *hollyhunt.com*

James Showroom *jamesshowroom.com*

Jane Shelton *janeshelton.com*

Katie Ridder *katieridder.com*

Kravet *kravet.com*

Lauren Hwang New York *laurenhwangnewyork.com*

Lee Jofa *kravet.com/lee-jofa*

Lisa Fine Textiles *lisafinetextiles.com*

Mally Skok *mallyskokdesign.com*

Marked NY *markedny.com*

Michael S. Smith *michaelsmithinc.com*

Perennials *perennialsfabrics.com*

Peter Dunham Textiles *peterdunhamtextiles.com*

Peter Fasano *peterfasano.com*

Quadrille *quadrillefabrics.com*

Raoul Textiles *raoultextiles.com*

Schumacher *fschumacher.com*

Supply Showroom *supplyshowroom.com*

Virginia Kraft *virginiakraft.com*

FURNITURE MAKERS

Billy Baldwin Studio *billybaldwinstudio.com*

Bunny Williams Home *bunnywilliamshome.com*

Carlos Moreno

Century Furniture *centuryfurniture.com*

Chaddock *chaddockhome.com*

David Sutherland *sutherlandfurniture.com*

Design Within Reach *dwr.com*

Flexform Modern Furniture *flexform.it/en*

Hickory Chair *hickorychair.com*

Highland House *highlandhousefurniture.com*

Hollywood at Home *hollywoodathome.com*

House + Town *houseandtown.com*

Janus et Cie *janusetcie.com*

Kerry Joyce *kerryjoyce.com*

Lawson-Fenning *lawsonfenning.com*

Ligne Roset *ligne-roset.com*

Made Goods *madegoods.com*

McGuire *bakerfurniture.com*

Oomph *oomphhome.com*

Paul Ferrante *paulferrante.com*

Roche Bobois *roche-bobois.com*

Serena & Lily *serenaandlily.com*

Soane Britain *soane.co.uk*

The Lacquer Company *thalacquercompany.com*

LIGHTING

Andrea Koeppel

Bevolo *bevolo.com*

Christopher Spitzmiller *christopherspitzmiller.com*

Coleen & Company *coleenandcompany.com*

Galerie des Lampes *galeriedeslampes.com*

Paul Ferrante *paulferrante.com*

Soane Britain *soane.co.uk*

Stephen Antonson *stephenantonson.com*

The Urban Electric Co. *urbanelectric.com*

Vaughan Designs *vaughandesigns.com*

Visual Comfort visualcomfort.com

LINENS

Biscuit Home *biscuit-home.com*

Julia B. *juliab.com*

Lettrefina Linens *www.etsy.com/shop/Lettrefina*

Matouk *matouk.com*

Serena & Lily *serenaandlily.com*

PAINT

Benjamin Moore *benjaminmoore.com*

Farrow & Ball *farrow-ball.com*

Sherwin-Williams *sherwin-williams.com*

PLUMBING & HARDWARE

Elegant Additions *elegantadditions.net*

Fixtures & Fittings *fixturesfittings.com*

Kohler *kohler.com*

Rohl *houseofrohl.com*

VOLA *en.vola.com*

Waterworks *waterworks.com*

RUGS

Elizabeth Eakins *elizabetheakins.com*

Fibreworks *fibreworks.com*

Holland & Sherry *hollandandsherry.com*

Kings House Oriental Rugs *kingshouseorientalrugs.com*

Matt Camron Rugs *mattcamron.com*

Patterson Flynn *pattersonflynn.com*

Rug Mart Houston *rugmarthouston.com*

Scout Design Studio *scoutdesignstudio.com*

STARK Carpet *starkcarpet.com*

SPECIALTY STORES

Paloma & Co *shoppalomaandco.com*

KRB NYC *krbnyc.com*

Hive Palm Beach *hivepalmbeach.com*

Mecox *mecox.com*

Bungalow Classic *bungalowclassic.com*

Jayson Home *jaysonhome.com*

STONE & TILE

Ann Sacks *annsacks.com*

Aria Stone Gallery *ariastonegallery.com*

Chateau Domingue *chateaudomingue.com*

Clé Tile *cletile.com*

Country Floors *countryfloors.com*

TRIMMINGS

Houlès *houles.com*

Samuel & Sons *samuelandsons.com*

WALLCOVERINGS

de Gournay *degournay.com*

Gracie *graciestudio.com*

Iksel *iksel.com*

Maya Romanoff *mayaromanoff.com*

Phillip Jeffries *phillipjeffries.com*

ACKNOWLEDGMENTS

WHEN IT COMES TO BRINGING an interior design project to fruition, it truly takes a village to get to the finish line. Working in collaboration with my team each day is one of the most rewarding aspects of being a designer. I am especially grateful to my Paloma Contreras Design team, both past and present, for keeping the needle moving forward every day. The past few years have been especially challenging in the design world. Your resilience, tenacity, hard work, love of design, and creativity are nothing less than inspiring. To my Paloma & Co team, thank you for making work so much fun!

We are very fortunate to collaborate with so many talented people—from architects to artists, artisans, and the most skilled workrooms. Your decades of experience and unparalleled artistry add immense beauty to our projects. You inspire me every day.

To the wonderful photographers whose work appears in this book— Brittany Ambridge, Carmel Brantley, and Aimee Mazzenga, whose work is featured chiefly throughout these pages—thank you for making my rooms sing. Aimee, you are the most incredible collaborator—thoughtful, immensely creative, and willing to do anything to get the shot! To Cate Ragan, my talented stylist—your flowers are the most beautiful and your energy is contagious! The way you see things inspires me. Aimee and Cate, I will forever treasure the memories of our adventures traveling all over the country to photograph these projects. Thank you for sharing your gifts—and so many laughs—with me!

To Kathryn O'Shea-Evans, thank you for capturing my voice so eloquently in these pages. You made writing this book both fun and deeply enriching. I know that your words will truly inspire the readers of this book.

To my literary agent, Berta Treitl, my editor, Rebecca Kaplan, and the entire team at Abrams, thank you for believing in me and allowing me the space to bring my creative vision to life.

To the editors who have been supportive of me and my work over the years—Dara Caponigro, Robert Rufino, Cynthia Frank, Carolyn Engelfield, Whitney Robinson, Newell Turner, Michael Boodro, Sophie Donelson, Hadley Keller, Carisha Swanson, Pamela Jaccarino, Amy Astley, Madeline O'Malley, Steele Marcoux, Jacqueline Terrebonne, Jill Waage, Ann Maine, and Margot Shaw—thank you for your encouragement and for taking my career to new heights.

To my parents, thank you for being my biggest cheerleaders and stepping in to be "the village" when this working mom must step away for work. I couldn't do it without your support.

To my amazing husband, Fabian, and our darling daughter, Margot: I would not be where I am without your love and unwavering support and enthusiasm. I love you both beyond measure.

Finally, a huge, heartfelt thank-you to my wonderful clients for allowing me the opportunity to work on your incredible projects. I am forever grateful for the trust you place in me and my team. This book is for you.

PALOMA CONTRERAS is an acclaimed interior designer and tastemaker based in Houston, Texas. Paloma's design sensibility is a modern take on traditional style—gravitating toward classic silhouettes and timeless pieces paired with a touch of glamour and an infusion of color. Paloma has honed her distinct eye over more than a decade in the design industry and a lifetime of appreciating beauty in all its various forms. She has developed a reputation for designing beautiful interiors in a broad range of styles, executed in a manner that is polished, refined, and effortless. Paloma's interiors are at once timeless and fresh—balancing attention to detail and the intersection of form and function to enhance a well-lived life.

Paloma and her work have been featured in numerous publications and websites, including *Elle Decor, Veranda, Architectural Digest, House Beautiful, Galerie, Vogue, Domino, Luxe, Traditional Home,* and *Town & Country*. Paloma recently debuted a lighting collection with Visual Comfort & Co. Her curated retail shop, Paloma & Co, opened in Houston's River Oaks neighborhood in January 2019 and has expanded to include a robust online platform. Paloma is currently working on projects in Houston and beyond, with clients in Palm Beach, Key Largo, Atlanta, New York City, and New Jersey.

OPPOSITE My client and I fell hard for this de Gournay wallpaper for their Palm Beach home: it's so fresh and tropical and has a metallic ground that supplies their great room with a lustrous glow.

Editor: Rebecca Kaplan
Designer: Sarah Gifford
Design Manager: Darilyn Carnes
Managing Editor: Lisa Silverman
Production Manager: Alison Gervais
Stylist: Cate Ragan

Library of Congress Control Number: 2023930560

ISBN: 978-1-4197-6297-0
eISBN: 979-8-88707-204-3

Printed and bound in China
10 9 8 7 6 5 4 3 2 1

Abrams books are available at special discounts when purchased
in quantity for premiums and promotions as well as fundraising
or educational use. Special editions can also be created to
specification. For details, contact specialsales@abramsbooks.com or
the address below.

ABRAMS
The Art of Books

195 Broadway
New York, NY 10007
abramsbooks.com